THE LIBRARY OF PRACTICAL THEOLOGY
General Editor : Martin Thornton

INCARNATION AND IMMANENCE

INCARNATION AND
IMMANENCE

by

HELEN OPPENHEIMER

HODDER AND STOUGHTON
LONDON SYDNEY AUCKLAND TORONTO

To the "Metaphysicals"

EDITORIAL PREFACE

There have been subtle changes since *The Library of Practical Theology* was launched in 1968. Things have settled down since the theological popularity, even vogue-ishness, of the mid sixties. But interest continues, less fashionable perhaps but more serious and at a deeper level. Doctrines of creation and redemption leading into ecology and environmental studies, a revolt against institutionalism, a continued reappraisal of Christian morality, above all the question of language and the doctrine of God: all this retains an obvious bearing on the peculiar problems facing contemporary society.

More than ever the institutional churches look to their laymen, no longer in merely administrative and financial capacities, but as leaders of thought and formulators of policy. The "simple layman who knows no theology", however wise and influential in other ways, is an anachronism. Theology means the Word of God – biblical, prophetic and incarnational – and although the responsible layman might justifiably jib at theology in its more rarefied moods, he can hardly disclaim interest in the Word of God. But theology ranges widely, and all Christians, clerical and lay, must seek their own theological level. That is the principle, or one principle, behind *The Library of Practical Theology*.

It is appropriate that this first volume of the new phase deals with the question of divine Immanence within the world, and of our experience of it. It is also appropriate that it is the work of a distinguished member of the laity.

MARTIN THORNTON

FOREWORD

This book is an attempt to take seriously a group of problems in philosophical theology concerning the relationships of people with God and each other. It has to do mainly with the question of Immanence, a subject which invites the old jibe about a small boy's watch: when it had been taken to bits and put together again, there seemed to be enough pieces left to make another.

I have incorporated parts of several articles by kind permission of the S.P.C.K. and the Editor of *Theology*. "The Identifying of Grace" (*Theology*, February 1965) has become the basis of Chapter III, and "Praying for Guidance" (*Church Quarterly Review*, July–September 1962) of Chapter V; while the whole book is really an expansion and development of "Immanence" (*Theology*, March 1966), bits of which appear throughout. (I have also used in Chapter IV a few paragraphs from an article on the Resurrection in *Theology*, March 1967).

I must apologise to the reader for the considerable number of quotations and references. Stylistically this is regrettable, but for my purpose it was needful, for reasons which should be apparent, especially in Chapter IX. I have not wanted to pursue these topics in isolation but in dependence upon, I should like to say even in a kind of community with, other people who have thought on these matters. But one cannot engage in discussion with other people if one is afraid to let them use their own words: the only result would be a sort of puppet play.

The making of acknowledgment is therefore peculiarly apt, and I am conscious of owing innumerable debts, most of which I hope will become apparent in the footnotes. I am particularly grateful to all the members, individually and collectively, of a group of theologians and philosophers which used to meet in Oxford under the name of the Metaphysicals; to Dr. Martin Thornton for setting me upon this pursuit and for his most helpful criticism of my manuscript at what turned out to be a very inconvenient time for him; to the Editor of *Theology*, Professor G. R. Dunstan, for much kind encouragement; to Professor Dorothy Emmet for constructive criticism and for introducing me to C. C. J. Webb in person and in his writings; and most of all to my husband for unfailing help and interest.

L.H.O.

Thanks are due to Messrs. Faber and Faber Ltd. for permission to quote from T. S. Eliot's *The Cocktail Party*; and to the Dacre Press (A. & C. Black Ltd.) for permission to use a passage from Austin Farrer's *The Glass of Vision*. Biblical quotations are taken from the American Revised Standard Version.

CONTENTS

THE PROBLEM

CHAPTER ONE

The Emperor's New Clothes

In Hans Andersen's story the Emperor was simply the victim of a fraud: an easy victim because of human dishonesty and conceit. No grown-up person was prepared to admit that the famous new clothes were invisible to him, as that would be to admit to stupidity or unsuitability for his office. When the fraud was exposed it was punctured like a balloon; for all that the Emperor, from courage or convention, decided to keep up appearances and go on with the procession.

Suppose the story were to be told another way, spoiling its clear outlines but taking a more lenient view of human nature. Some of the Emperor's subjects have had their doubts from the start, but do not want to ruin the occasion, from motives compounded no doubt of self-interest, laziness and kindliness. So they cast down their eyes as their Emperor goes by, or hide behind the flags and bunting and raise a muffled cheer. The single sharp intervention of the small child is replaced by an uneven pressure, a mingling of reactions: tactful, enthusiastic or incredulous. The balloon is not burst, and the Emperor goes back to his palace in a state of diffused unease. The sting of his situation is not exactly that he has made a fool of himself, but that he may after all be clad in the most glorious garments yet will never know this for certain. He can never find out whether he is indeed the victim of a fraud or not, unless he is prepared to take the risk of declaring his own vulnerability.

The application to religious language is obvious, and the diffused unease and undeclared vulnerability only too apparent. At such a juncture to play a part somewhat analogous to that of the small child, to look naively at certain Christian statements and begin to ask, in all

diffidence, what they amount to in fact and in detail, may
not be to show up the Emperor for a fool or a knave. One
might indeed help to promote appreciation for the
honestly fitted clothes he actually has on.

To take a more serious analogy; Christians ought to be
aware of the possibility of finding themselves in the
position of a frightened patient, who may not be seriously
ill, but who cannot believe this because he knows people
are often not told when they have cancer. To keep some
people in a fool's paradise, he is being deprived of the
chance of honourable comfort. Yet like the Emperor he
dares not ask where he really stands; and if he does ask
he has only uncertain criteria for weighing the sincerity
of the answer; and in the end the true answer may still
turn out to be what he dreads to hear.

Such a predicament once it has arisen can prove practically inescapable. There is the more reason then for
those concerned to try, if possible ahead of time, in a cool
hour, in patience rather than heroic desperation, to
approach the unfaceable question. In theology the disease
which is not to be named is meaninglessness, leading to
the "death by a thousand qualifications" as diagnosed by
Professor Flew.[1]

But, it will be said, the meaningfulness of religious
language is *the* problem of the philosophy of religion. Far
from being unmentionable, it has been discussed and
discussed until it is practically threadbare. This is so. Likewise cancer may seem to be *the* subject of medical research,
and of popular medical concern. Yet what I have tried
to characterise as the predicament of the Emperor's New
Clothes remains. For all the discussion, the question of
what specific religious statements amount to is apt to be
left hanging in the air.

In practice, while theologians pursue their studies on
the assumption that particular religious statements are
indeed meaningful, philosophers discuss what religious
language means in general. They have been greatly
exercised over two characteristic "philosophy of religion"
issues: the theory of analogy (If we cannot talk literally

---

[1] In "Theology and Falsification", a discussion in *University* reprinted in
New Essays in Philosophical Theology, p. 97, (S.C.M., 1955).

about God, how *can* we talk about Him?) and a version of the problem of evil (What can it mean to say there is a good God if nothing is to be allowed to falsify this?). Meanwhile the level of discussion at which the effective meaning of particular religious statements could constructively be questioned is commonly left by philosophers to theologians and by theologians to philosophers.

There seems no compelling reason for leaving this level undiscussed until the philosophers have concluded their debate on the meaningfulness of religious language in general, and sound reason for not so waiting, since the theologians are certainly not waiting and continue to make religious statements. To justify such statements *en bloc* would indeed be a magnificent enterprise, though not one to be undertaken lightly: but it is not necessarily the only way to think philosophically about religion. It need not be illegitimate to make a kind of interim assumption that religious language is or may be meaningful, and to try, while using this language with the theologians to say particular things, to enquire carefully what some of these specific statements amount to. Any theological illumination thrown by such enquiry will be that much gain in its own right, and the possibility of such illumination may contribute to some extent towards vindicating the meaningfulness of religious language in general.

It would be disingenuous not to acknowledge at once that it is the language of Christian doctrine which I have in mind. More particularly, there is a group of characteristic Christian theological statements where the Emperor's New Clothes difficulty, once attended to at all, is especially obtrusive. These statements are concerned with the theology of grace, and the problem to which they give rise can be roughly and provisionally identified by the label of "the concept of unity-in-plurality". Christians have a great deal to say about the ways in which people are or can be related to God and to each other, and many of the things they wish to say take for granted the possibility of certain sorts of close relationships which are not on the face of it compatible with common sense. They work with a characteristic concept of *personal immanence* which is often not made explicit and which is by no

2

means self-explanatory. They speak of persons "abiding in" one another, yet somehow remaining distinct. They say not only that they can know God and be known of Him but that His grace can enter into their own wills. To stop making some of these statements would be to stop being a Christian, but that does not make it the part of a Christian to utter such statements irresponsibly. Rather, if he is philosophically inclined, he is committed to the undertaking of trying to make some sort of viable whole out of his thinking.

To explore these matters is to study *philosophical theology*, in which the Christian philosopher must insist on being allowed to take into philosophical account theological data, in something like the way in which he is at present in the habit of taking into account psychological or physical data. The philosophical discussion of the problems of unity-in-plurality may be a task parallel to the philosophical discussion of, for example, the problem of perception. There is no need to stop first and delimit precisely where philosophy stops and the special science begins: that would be a further philosophical problem in its own right. The difficulties over the Christian application of the concept of immanence, like the difficulties over perception, are sufficient to invite our attention under whatever classification. In either case the study of the difficulties is worth while because in a particular area which one is prepared to take seriously, one is confronted with data which set the problem.

In the present case the data which set the problem are biblical. Traditionally, "philosophy of religion" has been thought bound to confine itself to matters of "natural theology". It is necessary to insist that "philosophical theology" ought not to be so bound. If for any reason we believe that the Bible and particularly the New Testament sets out a reputable system of thought (let alone believing it to offer the Way, the Truth and the Life), it becomes philosophically respectable to take that system *in its details* and see how it fits with the rest of our thinking. If the philosopher is going to shudder professionally at the idea of filling out theism with specific Christian theology, he will be putting the theologians into a game reserve of their own which he has barred himself from entering, and will be the only person to blame if philosophically wild things should go on there. It will be his fault if the theologians succumb, in Tillich's phrase, to "the danger of trying to fill in logical gaps with devotional material".[1]

The data in question here represent a whole aspect of biblical Christianity which is not so much neglected as undigested. On the one hand Christianity has been presented in a thoroughgoing way as the religion of the *individual*: the child of the heavenly Father, the soul to be saved, the lost sheep to be sought. Even the flock gathered in the sheepfold, however huddled together and however little endowed with minds of their own, remain separate entities. They know the shepherd and he knows them: there is no need yet to talk of "immanence".

Yet simply alongside this way of thinking, apparently not constructively integrated with it, is that whole other aspect of Christianity in which Christians are baptised into Christ and partake of his body; they are members of one another, branches of the vine; they minister to the unfortunate and find they have ministered to Christ; they abide in him and he in them; they declare that one died for all therefore all died; and of their Christian lives they say "not I but Christ liveth in me".

The oddity which calls for attention is not that Christian theologians are puzzled by this language so integral to the Christian faith, but that they seem so little puzzled. They use it indeed as if it were self-explanatory, as if it were an answer to other problems, not with an embarrassed air as if it were one of the harder parts of Christianity to render intelligible. An example is needed which is not an Aunt Sally but comes from a standard work. This is Bicknell on the Thirty-nine Articles: "It is just because Christ is more than a single human individual that His perfect humanity can be the source of new life to us. His death is not an act outside us".[2] Here is assuredly firmly based biblical Christianity: but it is a

---

[1] *Systematic Theology* Vol. 1, p. 118, (Nisbet, 1953).
[2] E. J. Bicknell, *The Thirty-nine Articles of the Church of England*, ed. H. J. Carpenter, p. 58, (Longmans, third edition, 1955).

good deal further than it looks from plain common-sense clarity.

For all this talk of unity is one pole, but only one pole, of what is fashionably called a "tension" in Christianity; and the odd thing is that this particular tension, the tension between the individual and the corporate, should seem to be so little felt. The problem is that in Christianity at its most characteristic the separate entities which we suppose ourselves to be, and which much of Christianity equally characteristically encourages us to believe ourselves to be, are often associated with the Deity and with each other in very mysterious ways. The difficulty is not to see how it makes sense for separate persons to become one, abandoning individualism altogether. Many thinkers of a pantheistic cast of mind seem to have had no difficulty in envisaging such a possibility and explaining fairly adequately to others what they mean. The difficulty is to see what kind of unity is at the same time compatible with a continuing and equally important distinction between persons. I can understand only too clearly how when the spirit returns to God who gave it it can be absorbed as a drop in the ocean. I can understand a religion, however unpalatable I might find it, which would tell me to accept this absorption and not resist it. But what am I to make of a religion which insists that we are indeed to become one with each other and with God while remaining distinct individuals? One would at least expect some difficult formula like the Athanasian creed in which the two apparently irreconcilable ways of thinking would be set alongside each other for one's adherence. It is surely not naive literalism to think this matter worthy of philosophical attention.

The question, briefly, is how the concepts of unity and distinctness can be held together *within the personalist way of thinking* to which one is committed by the very terms in which the problem has been set. It is assumed from the outset that the relationships between God and man are "personal" relationships. Such an assumption will gradually need to be both made more explicit and qualified. "Personalism" can mean many things, from a crude theological anthropomorphism whose God walks in the garden in the cool of the day, to a plain ethical humanism which judges moral problems by the satisfaction of people. For the present, it is enough to acknowledge a generally "personalist" approach, a way of thinking coloured by a tendency to see problems of all kinds in terms of persons and personal relationships.

This approach is compatible with the recognition that such an understanding may frequently in the course of the argument prove too simple and in need of refinement; but it is not compatible with any attempt to give up speaking of God in fully personal terms. The great biblical personal images of God, Father, King, Judge, Bridegroom, are far too prominent for the problems to be avoided, within an understanding that claims to be Christian, by treating them as expendable metaphors. If they are abandoned when the difficulties about unity begin to be felt, then there is no point in trying to understand the unity language either, for its setting is the language of God as personal.

To justify this starting point any further runs into the notorious difficulty of proving the obvious. Dr. Farrer was able to take the short way with the impersonalists and say bluntly that expressions like "ground of being" left him "in a perfect fog".[1] "One of the silliest of all discussions", he said, "is the question whether God is personal – it would be as useful to enquire whether ice is frozen. The theological question is . . . whether the world depends upon a supreme creative will; and that is the same thing as supreme person."[2] For those more timid, or more set upon being radical, it is worth pointing out that they have good precedent for remaining personalists. For example, neither in *Honest to God* nor in *Exploration into God* does Dr. Robinson wish to repudiate personalism, only to go beyond what he calls the theistic "projection".[3] He is well aware of the danger that "those who have aimed at a supra-personal Deity have ended more often than not with one that is less than fully personal".[4]

[1] *Faith and Speculation*, p. 46, (A. & C. Black, 1967).
[2] *Saving Belief*, p. 30, (Hodder and Stoughton, 1964).
[3] *Exploration into God*, p. 115, (S.C.M., 1967).
[4] ibid., p. 130.

At least once he is fully explicit: "I do not pray to the ground of my being. I pray to God as Father".[1]

What the Christian is taking for granted, defending, or hoping for when he counts himself a personalist need not be the existence of a God comfortably like himself, but a God with whom he can somehow or other enter into personal relationship. He will not be likely to be satisfied unless he can conceive this relationship as two-sided; unless, in C. C. J. Webb's phrase, there is or can be reciprocation.[2] This is the real point. Further discussion of divine personality is embroidery upon it.

To put the point so must be at once to put a large question mark beside it. Can the concept of a personal God stand up, not in opposition to the concept of an impersonal God, but in opposition to the idea that there is no God at all? Can there be any justification for transferring the kind of talk we readily use about ourselves and each other to a supposed transcendent being who differs from human beings in most fundamental respects? Is God "personal" in such a peculiar sense that we can build nothing definite upon it? Before there is any need to start asking how I can become one with God without losing my separate identity, I must ask difficult questions about whether I can have any idea of the "identity" of God at all. Unless God can first be posited, even to some extent recognised, as distinguishable from people,[3] the problem about unity-in-plurality is simply undercut. The New Testament "individualist" language does not for long seem easier to interpret than its "unity" language, and it will need somehow to be interpreted before the difficulty of reconciling them ever arises. The Emperor's New Clothes are evidently presented as a complete outfit, without which Christian theism will have practically nothing to wear at all, not just a warm and splendid outer garment to make him more comfortable and more magnificent.

[1] *The Honest to God Debate*, p. 262, (S.C.M., 1963). See also *Exploration into God*, p. 14.

[2] *God and Personality*, p. 70, (Allen & Unwin, 1918). Also *Pascal's Philosophy of Religion*, p. 32, (Oxford, 1929).

[3] cf. C. C. J. Webb, *Problems in the Relation of God and Man*, p. 139, (Nisbet, 1911).

CHAPTER TWO

Persons and Bodies

To consider the "identity" of God and the possibility of
finding oneself in personal relationship with Him is to
be compelled to explore an area where long-standing
philosophical uncertainty is variegated with patches of
overconfidence: for one cannot discuss the relationships
of persons without taking into account the embodied
condition of human persons, whether this condition be
accepted with enthusiasm or the reverse. To make any
progress here one has to start asking what a person is and
in particular what it can mean to say that a person is
"more" than a body; and for the religious believer the
question will arise of whether the traditional concept of
an individual immaterial spirit, human or divine, is
coherent in itself, necessary, and in accordance with the
facts. At some stages of human thought such a concept
seems to be based on common sense, at others to be
paradoxical or worse; but it seems both to be demanded
by and to create difficulties in most sorts of theology.
For the present problem the questions are particularly
insistent. In so far as we are bodily, can we be anything
other than separate discontinuous items in the world?
How can such separateness once established ever give
place to the kinds of unity of which Christianity tells?

Religious people have often and understandably wanted
to believe in the possibility of immaterial spirits because
they have wanted to believe in immortal souls, and this
issue has been allowed to spread out and sometimes
almost conceal all the others. A Christian ought to be in a
fairly strong position for containing it within bounds again,
as he is not in fact committed to believe that what lives
for ever is an immortal soul at all; it is the resurrection
of the dead for which he looks, not their automatic survival.

He has no need to wage war against "materialism" for he is not interested in shadowy ghosts and is proud of being some kind of materialist himself.

But this containment of the "survival" issue should be in order to face the whole problem, not to take the opportunity to run away from it. The primary question, which includes but goes beyond the matter of an after life, is not the detachability of the soul but the nature of a person and the relationships of which a person is intrinsically capable. To think in terms of relationships is in line with the reply of Christ to the Sadducees,[1] that the God of Abraham, Isaac and Jacob is not the God of the dead but of the living. What needs to be asked is, of what kinds of beings, capable of entering into what kinds of relationships, can this be affirmed? The bodies with which Abraham, Isaac and Jacob saw and heard and talked and acted have long ago disappeared into the earth; the God whom they served is traditionally characterised as a spirit without body, parts or passions; yet somehow they live, alive with His life. To pose the problem in this way makes it more needful not less to take a critical look at the concepts of embodiment and disembodiment.

"We have" said Locke, "as clear a perception and notion of immaterial substance as we have of material".[2] There is irony here: it is equal obscurity rather than equal clarity which he is claiming; but there is no unmanageable scepticism. Immaterial substance has been through centuries of human thought a thoroughly respectable concept. Nor has it been idly taken for granted, creeping in unnoticed at first as misconceptions have a way of doing. Rather it has consolidated its status by intellectual struggles.

The doubt about it can be brought to a head by taking one famous struggle as an example and asking bluntly whether after all the problem does not remain more vivid than the solution. St. Augustine of Hippo had the greatest difficulty in winning through from a kind of would-be "advanced" rarified materialism to a doctrine of entirely immaterial spirit. When he came to Milan

[1] Mark 12: 18-27.
[2] *Essay* II; XXIII; 15.

he was bowled over by the discovery that Ambrose and
his fellow Catholics did not after all teach a grossly
material doctrine of a God bounded by a human form.[1]
"The story", says his biographer,[2] "which Augustine
tells in the *Confessions* of his dilemmas in dealing with the
problem is one of the most dramatic and massive evocations
ever written of the evolution of a metaphysician; and
his final 'conversion' to the idea of a purely spiritual
reality, as held by sophisticated Christians in Milan, is a
decisive and fateful step in the evolution of our ideas on
spirit and matter."

But still, surely, his earlier doubts have relevance.
"When I desired to meditate on my God", he says,[3]
"I did not know what to think of but a huge extended
body – for what did not have bodily extension did not
seem to me to exist – and this was the greatest and almost
the sole cause of my unavoidable errors." "I had, thus
far", he explains candidly, "no conception of mind,
except as a subtle body diffused throughout local spaces."
To such naivety, once exposed, there can be no return,
and Augustine himself expected to be smiled at, "blandly
and lovingly" for it. But what one is still in no position
to smile at is the problem which occasioned the naivety.
How indeed is a Christian to set about meditating upon
his God? What content can he give to the idea of a spirit
if spatial terms are to be ruled out? It is still not obvious
how, without St. Augustine's magnificent religious
experience,[4] he is to shake himself free of St. Augustine's
difficulty: "For whatever I conceived to be deprived of
the dimensions of space appeared to me to be nothing,
absolutely nothing; . . . nor could I see that the act of
thought, by which I formed those ideas, was itself
immaterial."[5]

Unfortunately recent philosophical thinking has tended
to show St. Augustine only too right in hesitating to
divorce the idea of a person from the necessity of having
a foothold in the world of space. The best way to take

[1] *Confessions* VI: 111.
[2] Peter Brown, *Augustine of Hippo*, pp. 84–6, (Faber, 1967).
[3] *Confessions* V: 10.
[4] e. g. *Confessions* VII, X and XVII.
[5] ibid. VII: 1.

hold of a philosophical problem is often to think out into its details what one has supposed one could imagine. The concept of a disembodied spirit seems reasonably easy to imagine, and much fiction, let alone philosophy, is based upon it; but when one tries to pursue it seriously one is apt to find that one has really been thinking of a sort of rarified bodily being, like a cinema ghost, perhaps transparent, perhaps with strange powers of going through closed doors or vanishing, but certainly not completely disembodied. Here St. Augustine may smile "blandly and lovingly" at us, not we at him.

To put it another way, one may ask, What difference would it make to me here and now if I were disembodied? At least there is no need to go too fast here. The question is anyway significant enough to distinguish itself initially from the question, What difference would it make to me if I were dead? To die is to come to a stop, to lose consciousness, to leave this world altogether, perhaps to wake up somewhere else; and we do not in fact identify ourselves so closely with our bodies that "disembodiment" has all that as part of its meaning. Those philosophers who take the short way with "the soul", identifying persons with people and people with animated bodies,[1] do not start with common sense on their side. We are at least able to make a beginning in thinking our bodies away and supposing our "selves" to be still there. We can even ask the question whether death itself is after all "only" disembodiment. Perhaps when somebody dies he does not "lose consciousness", in spite of the behaviour of his body, but hangs about on the scene: Charles Williams describes death in these terms in more than one of his novels.

If "conscious disembodiment" is nonsense then it is subtle nonsense, worth enquiring into, not like "square circle". Here I sit at my desk: suddenly I am disembodied: what do I lose? Let us for simplicity suppose my body not to have slumped down insensate but to have vanished away. My hand was on the desk: I can no longer see it, nor feel any bodily sensation. I cannot pick up my pen and fiddle with it; worse, I cannot pick up my pen and

[1] See below, p. 31 note 2.

write with it. Nor can I communicate with other people
by speech, having neither tongue, lips nor vocal chords.
Unless by some physical miracle I am allowed to influence
the sound waves affecting their ears, I shall have to
occupy myself with my own resources, not with human
conversation. Can I hear what other people say, or listen
to music? The idea that I could is not immediately
inconceivable, but has a difficulty: which sounds will
I hear, of all the noises going on in the world? One thing
our ears do for us is pick up the particular sound waves
impinging on a particular spot. My body was indeed at a
particular spot, sitting at my desk. Perhaps that is where
"I" am still, but am I fixed there for ever? What would
it be like, now, for me to move away from one place to
another? I have accepted that I can no longer see my
hand on my desk: but can I see my desk? I have no retina
on which its image can appear.

It may sound, and indeed it may be, unimaginatively
literalist to ask how I can see without a retina, somewhat
like Nicodemus asking how he can be born again when he
is old; but what is absolutely needful to ask about sight
as just now about hearing, is how I can experience
without a *point of view*. As Professor MacIntyre put it in an
article in *Mind*,[1] "Where there is no body how is the
visual field limited? . . . Vision that had no location would
presumably be vision of everything and this is a notion to
which no meaning can be attached. To see everything
would entail being able to see through everything as well
as being able to see it." Dr. Shoemaker in *Self-Knowledge
and Self-Identity*[2] effectively uses a similar argument "to
show that it is senseless to suppose that there could be a
kind of seeing, or a kind of perception like seeing, that
does not involve the perceiver's having a body *some* part
of which plays the role that in ordinary vision is played
by the eyes."

This way of thinking indeed has nowadays become
commonplace among professional philosophers, but needs
to be garnered out of the philosophical books and periodi-
cals and forced upon the attentions of the theologically

[1] "A Note on Immortality", *Mind*, (1955), p. 398.
[2] p. 174ff, (Cornell, 1963).

minded, lest they should still suppose that so long as
crude materialism can be rejected, a Christian understanding of personality and the relationship of persons is
easy to defend. The philosophical discussion has mainly
been conducted in terms of the problem of how a person
is to be *identified*, by himself or by others. "I do not know",
insists Professor Hampshire,[1] "how I would identify
myself as a disembodied being, and I do not know what
this hypothesis means." It seems only common sense to
point out, as he does, that "I can only be said to have lost
a sense of my own identity if I have lost all sense of where
I am and what I am doing,"[2] but the implications for
this for the concept of a completely disembodied being,
who has lost his foothold of where he is and his ability
to do anything in the physical world, are distinctly
discouraging.

The case has been classically put and a theological
application actually made by Professor Strawson.[3] His
argument is the more telling as he does not overstate it.
He does not brush aside the possibility of identifying a
disembodied being, but shows how gravely attenuated
such a concept is, putting his finger on the solitariness of
such an individual: he can never find out "whether there
are any other members of his class". As a former person
"he is now debarred from entering into any of those
transactions the past fact of which was the condition of
his having any idea of himself at all . . . He must live
much in the memories of the personal life he did lead."
As his memories fade, he will gradually lose "his concept
of himself as an individual". "Disembodied survival, on
such terms as these, may well seem unattractive. No
doubt it is for this reason that the orthodox have wisely
insisted on the resurrection of the body."

The orthodox at this point may feel like saying "I told
you so," especially as B. H. Streeter in an essay published
in 1917[4] made the very point that consciousness needs a
localised centre. St. Paul himself clearly found the

[1] *Thought and Action*, p. 50, (Chatto & Windus, 1959).
[2] ibid., p. 75.
[3] *Individuals*, pp. 115-6, (Methuen, 1959).
[4] "The Resurrection of the Dead", *Immortality*, pp. 101-2, (Macmillan).

thought of disembodied survival unattractive.[1] It is worth insisting that characteristic Christian theology has always been concerned with the whole man as an embodied being, rather than with the unstable association of soul and body as two awkward units, into which it is easy for would-be spiritual thought to slide. But still complacency is by no means in order. Professor Strawson's ironical nod to the orthodox is as it were a swallow which does not make a summer. His understanding of what personal identity involves, though far subtler and more flexible than the kind of crude materialism which practically identifies people with their bodies, is not obviously compatible with much of what Christian theologians want to say about the links there can be between persons; and more particularly it is not obviously compatible with most of what Christian theologians want to say about God. If God is the disembodied spirit *par excellence* it is essential, in reverence not in irreverence, to make an effort to understand a little more fully what this could mean and how we could ever come to know Him.

Let it be said first that should the attempt fail the existence of God may be impugned but is not disproved. Intellectual argumentation is seldom ultimately convincing and ought not to have the last word either way. There have been people whose conviction of the reality of God has had a directness and power not easily explained away: for instance, Amos, Jeremiah, Paul, Augustine, Aquinas (who came in the light of experience to see his own magisterial analysis as no more than straw). These men are all associated with books: not because God is better known to the learned, but because dead servants of God are better known to us when they have left written works. It is also true that they all belong to the Judaio-Christian tradition, and this is fair criticism. Other names, perhaps Akhnaten, notably Mohammed, should be added, and the testimony would become conflicting, though perhaps less so than one might expect. The main point stands that the concept of God has meant too much to too many conspicuously effective human beings to be readily snuffed out as meaningless, however ineptly it

[1] II Cor. 5: 1–4.

may sometimes be interpreted by those who come afterwards. In these circumstances a proper task for the
theologian is the task Locke set himself as a philosopher,
of being an under-labourer to clear the ground a little,
in order to remove impediments from the paths of those
who have no overwhelming experience of their own to
steer by. If he fails, many may be hindered, including
probably himself; but a reasonable hope that the obstacles
after all are capable of being cleared away by somebody
more competent is not necessarily rendered illegitimate.

A constructive approach may be to look at the positive
not just the negative side of what might be called the
Strawson approach. For Professor Strawson, "person" is
a primitive or basic concept, which includes from the
start *both* states of consciousness and corporeal characteristics.[1] Dead bodies and disembodied persons are alike
secondary concepts.[2] The justification of this refusal to
separate body and mind is not a dubious argument from
bodily behaviour to concealed mental goings-on, but a
Kantian assurance that for us to have the experience we
do have, nothing less than the full material and mental
concept of a person will suffice. The person is indeed more
than the body, but once let this "more" get detached from
the body which gives it a point of reference and we shall
have great and unnecessary difficulty in catching it again.

The benefit of looking at the idea of disembodiment
by means of this approach is that it gives us an enlivened
understanding of what bodies are for. They are essentially
the point of contact of the person with his world, and
this remains true however widely we understand "world".
If we are only concerned with the physical world, then
the physical body is good enough for us; if we want to
postulate a spiritual world, then we must be ready to
postulate some kind of spiritual body. In either case, the
idea of a "point of contact" must work both ways.
Our bodies are the means by which we are identified and
they are at the same time the means by which we act
in our environment. This is not just something that happens
to be so, as rice happens to be the staple diet of large

[1] e.g., pp. 101–2.
[2] p. 103.

areas of the world. It is what "body" primarily signifies; as food is so to say the staple diet of all areas of the world. To talk about bodies in this way is by no means unbiblical; for example, Dr. J. A. T. Robinson in discussing the meaning of *soma* says that it can be understood as a man's "personality as materially and socially continuous with his environment."[1]

But, it may be asked, is this argument moving too fast? Are bodily criteria really so essential for the recognition of persons? Need we identify a person quite so closely with the body he happens to have? There has been a good deal of inconclusive philosophical argument lately about whether it makes sense to imagine that two people have "changed bodies". Suppose for a moment that they could: at once one realises that the "person" one is interested in, whose whereabouts one would want to find out, is a particular consciousness and character, not a bodily appearance after all. If such a peculiar situation could arise, one would surely stick to "personality" criteria of identity and say the two had changed bodies, rather than to the "same body" criterion which would oblige one to say that they had changed personalities; and if so, surely the "real person" is an immaterial being after all?

On the other hand, it is urged that the whole idea of such a change is incoherent, in that people's bodies are much more integral to their identity than the "personality" criterion allows.[2] The ways people speak or smile or frown or walk or tire themselves out or recover from illnesses are part of themselves and cannot be switched around. This is convincing but not quite conclusive. We might still say that likewise the way people wear out the elbows of their coats or ladder their stockings is part of themselves, and that a change of body would be like a very radical change of clothes, bringing incongruities but not impossibilities. Someone else's body would fit much less well than

---

[1] *In the End, God*, p. 85, (James Clarke & Co., 1950); cf. Leenhardt, "This is my Body", *Essays on the Lord's Supper*, p. 41, (Lutterworth Press, English translation, 1958).

[2] See e.g., B. A. O. Williams, "Personal Identity and Individuation", *Proceedings of the Aristotelian Society* (1956–7), printed in *Essays in Philosophical Psychology*, ed. Gustafson, (Macmillan, 1967). A. Flew, "Locke and the Problem of Personal Identity", *Philosophy* (1951), p. 59.

someone else's shoes, but is it utter nonsense to say that one might suddenly catch a glimpse of George's smile somehow filling out Henry's long countenance?

The argument is as "academic" as any argument could be, but it may have served to bring out the point that although we need not identify persons *with* their bodies we do and must identify them *by* their bodies. Whichever way the argument goes it remains true that the body one has at any given moment is one's means of contact with the world. If constant changes were the rule the body would be a maddeningly inefficient means, but we should still be dependent upon it. As Mr. A. M. Quinton has put it,[1] it would be a laborious business finding out where one's family and friends were, and human life would resemble an unending sequence of shortish ocean trips. Fortunately continuity *is* the rule, and we are not at the moment called upon to ascertain whether this is so necessarily or not.

All this has led up to a view of a *person* not as a dual being with detachable soul and body, but as, so to say, a living point of view, embodied in the world at a particular place and so able to know and be known, to move about and do things. An advantage of this view is that it does not prematurely define the limits of the person. What I call "I" is the being that thus impinges upon the world: I can shrink the idea of myself to a kind of bare consciousness or enlarge it to include more or less of the little domain from which I operate: my body, my clothes, my spectacles, my pen, my motor car can all be parts of "myself" in a hardly metaphorical sense. When my domain overlaps with other domains I may start to say "we" not just "I"; and almost at once the intricacies of "you" and perhaps "thou", "he", "she", "it" and "they" will have to be included in the picture.

The problems which arise about the ways in which persons understood after this fashion can be related to one another, the kinds of oneness and otherness which are possible for them, and the function of the material world of both uniting them and dividing them from one another, are immense and absorbing, not least in their theological

[1] In a lecture as far as I know unpublished.

aspects. But such problems about embodied persons are in a way manageable. The Christian has on his hands first of all a problem about the idea of God which cannot be evaded in would-be humility. If it is part of the meaning of a person to be known and to act through a body, is the concept of a personal but immaterial God ruled out? Is the living God of the Bible no more than an intolerably crude piece of anthropomorphism, so that there remains only a choice between atheism and the affirmation of some kind of "ground of being" which is in no proper sense personal? These are difficult matters and of course humility is in place; but not the kind of humility which closes its mind to the difficulty and can only assert unthinkingly that because God is spirit He does not need a body.[1] Such a way of thinking can seriously attenuate even if it does not utterly undermine our conception of God.[2]

God if He is real must indeed be different from men; but not by lacking something which human beings have. If one tries to imagine Him as a bodiless personal being one is forced on into denying Him any foothold in the world. It is more constructive tentatively and reverently to enquire what analogue there could be for God to the role of the physical body in our lives. If it is proper to look on our bodies as our points of contact with the world, so that an embodied person is a kind of living point of view, it is necessary for the believer in a personal God to wrestle with the notion of an infinite point of view. Such a notion might be self-contradictory, it may be pantheistic, but it is anyway not restrictive. To worship such a God would stretch not cramp one's mind.

Should the idea be self-contradictory it would be for the reason given by Professor MacIntyre: "Vision that had no location would presumably be vision of everything and this is a notion to which no meaning can be attached".[3] He is surely right that, for a finite being, vision which is not vision from a specific physical place is nonsense.

[1] The problem of how angels traditionally conceived as finite immaterial spirits could identify one another is acute: but belief in God cannot stand or fall by the conceivability of angels.

[2] cf. G. Ernest Wright, *God who acts*, p. 23, (S.C.M., *Studies in Biblical Theology*, No. 8, 1952).

[3] See above, p. 27.

3

But is it nonsense to suggest that somehow for an infinite being all points of view might be, so to speak, assembled; that the divine "vision" would not be from no place but from all places?[1] This seems to be what one does dimly imagine of God, if only one can break free from the potent childish and egocentric picture of a supernatural Eye in the sky looking down encouragingly or wrathfully upon one's own doings.

Is the idea of an infinite point of view essentially pantheistic? This need not necessarily condemn it, as C. C. J. Webb was wont to insist with a bad pun of Carlyle's: "What if it be Pot-theism, so it be true?" There is indeed a kind of pantheism which Christian theism must repudiate, in which the whole universe is looked upon as itself God; but pantheism of this kind is not here in question. Nor have we reverted to the ancient and crude picture of the universe as a body of which God is the soul, though here we are getting a little warmer. Both these views sink God in the universe rather than relating Him to it. What needs to be said, whether it sounds pantheistic or not, is that He must be related to the physical world at *all* points: the divine point of view is not single but infinite.

The question of pantheism must later recur;[2] for the present the next problem is how such "relation" of God to the world, even if we have some notion of it, can be anything but abstract. Bodies are not only points of view. They are for being known and for doing things: they are, one might say, vehicles or bearers of personality. What vehicle is available to God, if the concept of divine personality is not to be pathetically attenuated? When the question is put like this rather than in terms of "bodiless being" it does not seem so unanswerable. All the evidence we have for believing in God at all suggests that He has many vehicles, which bear His personality and reveal it in many ways and in many degrees.

Here a Christian will want to hurry on and emphasise the Word made flesh: the Incarnate Son, God literally

---

[1] I am indebted here to a suggestion made by Mr. John Lucas in discussion, that God's point of view could be "the class of all points of view".

[2] e.g. pp. 51f, 117, 127, 197ff, 201ff.

taking to Himself a body. This is indeed the direction in which the argument has been tending, but it is important to remember that the Incarnation cannot be the whole of the answer. One must have some concept of God already, to attach any sense to the words "God was in Christ". Historically Christ came, not to religious barbarians but to the most theologically sophisticated people of all. He transformed not instilled the idea of God. Those of us who come after have good reason to found our apologetic upon him,[1] but we can only believe because of Christ if it already made sense to entertain the notion of God without him. For it to be *God* who speaks to us by His Son He must be capable of speaking to us also "at sundry times and in divers manners"; otherwise it adds nothing extra to the idea of Jesus of Nazareth to call him Jesus Christ.

Nor must it be entirely metaphorical to say that God has many "vehicles". We are not just discussing aspects of the world which remind us of God or make us think, "Perhaps there is a God after all"; as a scent may recall to us a place we have once visited or a friendly strange dog make us think of a friend who owns one like him. We are discussing or trying to discuss God Himself in his physical manifestation, the actual equivalent for God of the physical bodies of His creatures.

It is surely legitimate to understand "God Himself" in the widest sense we used for persons[2] which included their clothes, their pens, their motor cars and not only their "bare consciousness". We cannot approach the idea of God's "bare consciousness"; but we must approach the idea that He truly impinges upon the material world by using real, physical points of contact. The heavens declare the glory of God; the prophets speak His word; the way we treat the hungry, the sick and the prisoners is the way we treat Christ; the Church and the sacraments are in different senses his Body. The present contention is that these statements are no less literal than "I ran out of petrol" or "I published an article", if God is sufficiently "embodied" to count as truly personal.

Yet they still seem less literal. I have tried to ease the

[1] See below, pp. 60, 62.
[2] See above, p. 32.

problem by blurring the boundaries between the human being and his immediate environment, to show that what we call "I" can have a wide spread, from brain and eyes to hands and feet, to nails and hair, to clothes, to belongings, to casual implements. I believe that to broaden in this way the concept of human identity does considerably ease the problem of talking meaningfully about divine identity; but in all honesty it must be admitted that it does not abolish it. It remains true that in the case of human beings we have a definite "core", so to speak, for each cluster of statements about what a person does, and this "core" consists of statements about what the person's body does. Each of us has a mysterious but quite specific primary relationship with his own body, and it is by means of one's own body that one is able to adopt other bodies for one's purposes. We can say that we *are* our bodies and so to speak *wield* other physical things. The difficulty in the case of God is that unless we can find a body for Him to *be* all talk of His *wielding* other bodies seems to be infected with metaphor.

The problem is deeply obscure but some light may be let into it by taking seriously the ideas, difficult enough in themselves but illuminating here, of God as infinite and God as creator: the idea of infinity to detach Him from the need to have a specific body, the idea of creation to relate Him to the world after all.

Of course the idea of an infinite being is opaque: so opaque that one cannot be sure it will not turn out to be self-contradictory. I have been suggesting though that for present purposes "being" can be explored in terms of "point of view". Though the concept of "infinite being" inevitably remains opaque, it becomes possible, or at least seems possible, to set up a significant contrast between a finite point of view, embodied and operating at a point in space, and an infinite point of view for which all points in space are "assembled".[1] One cannot understand but one can seem to see why one cannot understand, why one would not expect to locate the "core" of God's operations in this world in the way one locates oneself and other people.

[1] See above, p. 34.

But God's infinity cannot be the whole story, for it is not enough just to say that we cannot locate God at a particular place. People do claim to locate the activity of God: "God spoke" (by the mouth of the prophet Isaiah) is not supposed to be totally different from "Professor X published a book" (by his usual publishers). The trouble is that the second of these statements goes back quite straightforwardly to the author's physical exertion of writing and can claim to be a literal, though somewhat compressed, statement of fact; whereas the first statement has no such ready foothold in the physical world. Isaiah speaks by Isaiah's mouth. There is no room, except by metaphor, to say that the speaker is really God, and we can hardly found a faith on metaphor alone. It is all very well to say that the pantheist is "getting warm" if he pictures the whole universe as a body of which God is the soul;[1] but how warm is he getting? His picture is too crude to be taken literally; but if it is all we have to give God a primary relationship with physical reality, does not any talk of God "wielding" other bodies leave sense and truth very far behind?

But of course God has a "primary relationship" with physical reality, with every part of physical reality: He created it. Nothing could be more primary than that. It is not necessary to comprehend the meaning of creation to see that the notion is what is needed here. It enables us to say about God's "purchase on the world" something equivalent to what we have to say about a finite person's "purchase on the world". A finite being is a finite point of view, looking on the world from a particular place, and operating in the world by means of a very peculiar and mysterious relationship with a particular cluster of matter. Some philosophers would hold that the relationship is one of identity, that people *are* bodies; but at least they are a special sort of body, an animated body. Without claiming to understand either infinity or creation one can then move on to say something like this: just as God has an infinite, not a particular, point of view, so He has a peculiar and mysterious relationship, as it were like

---

[1] See above, p. 34.

"animating" but more so, with *every* cluster of matter.[1]
Such a conception does not sink God in the world.
It is technically "panentheism"[2] rather than theism:
that is, "The belief that the Being of God includes and
penetrates the whole universe, so that every part of it
exists in Him, but . . . that His being is more than, and is
not exhausted by, the universe".[3] Nor does such a view
imply that God "needs" the world in a sense unacceptable
to Christian belief: only that He needs the physical to
reveal Himself to physical beings. Granted that He has a
literal though admittedly unfathomable relationship, not
with one body as we do but with all bodies, one need not
get lost in metaphor by going on to say that, as we do,
He can "wield" any body that is available, identify
Himself with it, use it to act in His world and communicate with His creatures. "He who made the eye, shall he
not see?".[4]

A major objection at once arises. Here, it seems, not
with our families and friends, we really are in the "change
of body" situation. Forthwith the genuine difficulties of
this so far imagined situation become apparent. We do
not, unless we are idolaters, identify God with His physical
manifestations; our trouble is to identify Him *by* them,
when by common consent they are so exceedingly diverse.
How are we to distinguish the voice of God from the
voice of the false prophet, the grace of God from a sunny
day or a good digestion?

Worse: if one's thought is coloured by personalism[5] one
will want to emphasise that a truly personal God will
deal with His creatures personally. Surely then we
ourselves are His main point of contact with the world?
But if this is so, ought it not to be more obvious to us?
To what extent are we actually aware of when and how
He is impinging upon our lives, when He is using us as

[1] In all this I am greatly indebted to Austin Farrer's chapter on "The
God of Nature" in *A Science of God?* (e.g., pp. 74 and 83) Bles, 1966,
though I do not know whether he would have approved of what I have
made of his analysis.
[2] See below, p. 198.
[3] *Oxford Dictionary of the Christian Church*. See also J. A. T. Robinson,
Exploration into God, e.g., p. 83.
[4] Psalm 94.
[5] See above, pp. 20–1.

His "vehicles", when He is speaking to or through us?

In our situation, any enquiry into the character of the personal relationships possible between man and God must concern itself, at least at the outset, with this problem of identification. Such and such a relationship is said to occur: to ask what this statement amounts to is in effect to ask how to recognise the relationship when it does occur. It is in a way to ask for credentials, not necessarily in any sceptical or faithless spirit. If two strangers are to meet, they must have some arrangement for identifying each other, however trustful their approach. If someone is no stranger, one knows how to point him out to others. Likewise if people are to enter upon or continue in the Christian faith, they need some means of recognising what Christian language applies to their situation.

"Every moderately pious person feels *some* beginnings of the 'ligature' ", says Dom John Chapman.[1] "The reader is invited to direct his mind to a moment of deeply-felt religious experience, as little as possible qualified by other forms of consciousness", says Otto.[2] "All this day thy hand had led me", says a favourite hymn. Again, these are not Aunt Sallies. They are responsibly propounded and deserve to be taken seriously. Nor are they untypical of the kind of thing religious people want to say. Yet it is surely not only in the irreverent that these variegated approaches to the grace of God have a common tantalising quality, or even a tendency to induce a kind of alarmed paralysis. What would, so to say, meet or fail to meet such specifications? How are these relationships to be identified? It is not safe just to assume that one's own inadequacy is balanced by someone else's adequacy.

Of course it is in order for individual Christians to be totally inarticulate; nor are people to be expected to judge their own spiritual condition; but it is not an exorbitant demand that at least some members of the Christian Church should be prepared to try to explain, for instance, what would make it true or false to say "I live, yet not I but Christ . . .". How is the grace of God, His impinging upon the world, to be identified?

[1] *Spiritual Letters*, p. 90, (Sheed & Ward, New Ark Library, 1959).
[2] *The Idea of the Holy*, p. 8, (Oxford, 1950).

CHAPTER THREE

The Identifying of Grace

Thinking philosophically about grace is even harder than thinking philosophically about self-consciousness. It is like trying to see one's way with only the light of Professor Ryle's torch, the one that "illuminates itself by beams of its own light reflected from a mirror in its own insides".[1] One would hardly expect the grace of God to be a manageable topic; but most unmanageable topics are outside us and can be nibbled at, or at least surveyed. This unmanageable topic has its seat just where we can least get at it, within ourselves, and yet elusively beyond us as well. To know oneself is hard enough, but to know God within oneself is far harder. Purposely to direct one's attention to the problem of how God impinges upon one is like hunting short-sightedly for one's own spectacles. One needs God's grace to discern God's grace, and how can this circle first be broken? Yet if one is radically uncertain how to start looking for Him at the point of contact with one's own life, is there much sense in looking further afield?

Of course "radically uncertain" is strong language. It may be asked, how dare a practising Christian claim to be "radically uncertain" how to find God? To talk like this seems to deny centuries of Christian experience. Reverent agnosticism is all very well, but is there not a point at which for a Christian it becomes irresponsible agnosticism?

Unfortunately we are not in a position to take "centuries of Christian experience" for granted. Broadly speaking, Christians claim to be able to discern God at work in human life while admitting that there is room for error in individual cases; but we cannot always speak broadly.

[1] *Concept of Mind*, p. 194, (Hutchinson, 1949).

The grace of God surely does not work like a statistical average, only reliable if applied to a sufficiently large field. If it is at all what we take it to be it must have specific application. If it is so elusive that we can never actually say "Here it is: this is the work of God" the concept has been eroded out of recognition. Yet to give first-hand examples of grace, to single out instances that I am prepared to use with some precision to show someone else what I am trying to talk about, is both morally and logically presumptuous. I may say, "By the grace of God I am what I am" or "I could not have done this without God", but I dare not say "*This* is what God did in me". Even though Christians refrain from judging me proud, philosophers and psychologists will certainly judge me ill-advised.

It is common at this point to address oneself to a somewhat different problem, a problem difficult indeed but less fundamental than the one I am trying to pick out. There are after all plenty of standard examples of God's grace at work, from the conversion of St. Paul downwards. People are constantly making claims to have experienced grace in their own lives or to have recognised it in others. Granted these claims, it becomes important to decide how they are to be interpreted, theologically or otherwise, and what criteria are valid for their authentication; just as once we know who Raphael was, it becomes meaningful to try to find out whether a certain picture was painted by him or not. A model of such discussion is Professor Basil Mitchell's article on "The grace of God" in *Faith and Logic*.[1] He takes as a datum "the sense of a power at work in oneself or in others"[2] and so is confronted by "the challenge to explain the logical features of this sort of language".[3] His answer, very roughly, is that "saintliness"[4] is a discernible characteristic which cannot be separated from the notion of "God-dependence". If this quality impresses us sufficiently it will "impel us in the direction

[1] Allen & Unwin, 1957.
[2] p. 152.
[3] p. 151.
[4] p. 172.

of the supernatural"[1] and the Christian doctrine of grace legitimately comes in to offer us an interpretation of it.

But as he points out, "To the reader who protests that he has no such experience the argument of this chapter has nothing to say; he offers no purchase to it".[2] Suppose we want to begin by asking, not how to interpret such an experience but how to discern it? Suppose we are doubtful whether we have it or not, how can we make sure? Put like that, the problem may at first sound merely subjective and psychological, but it is, on the contrary, the *logical* problem of how we are to pick out what we are supposed to be discussing. Before a claim can be justified, it must be made. When are we to start to make it? Begin with the concept of grace, and we can go on to give it factual backing by recognising holiness in the great saints and acknowledging that this quality points beyond itself to something higher; but are we thereby any nearer to "identifying" grace in the sense I have tried to indicate? How are we to apply this somewhat general idea specifically enough to be of any use, and in particular how is it to be applied to the case that in the last resort ought to be most real, one's own actual or potential relationship with God?

It may well be felt that to indulge in this kind of worry is to make too much fuss about the difficulty of finding what we are looking for when it is nearest to us. Perhaps this problem of identifying grace is merely a special case of a very commonplace difficulty which is practical, not philosophical? "The eye sees not itself", clear self-knowledge is notoriously hard, doctors cannot easily treat themselves, and so on. Is it not quite natural that we should be able to pick out divine grace where it is outside ourselves and conspicuous, as in the great saints, and find it difficult to the point of impossibility to identify it in ourselves where it is much too near and on a much smaller scale?

If grace were a commodity or a mechanism this argument might settle one's doubts. It is only if it is

[1] p. 173.
[2] p. 152.

to be defined in terms of personal relationship that it will never do to say that we can only expect to see it clearly in others. But then we constantly do define or at least illustrate grace in terms of relationship, and it must be admitted that the standard analogies by which we do this are far from soothing in the present context. If a child were expected to learn from other children's relationships with their parents what a father or mother could be or if a husband or wife began to say that one could only understand what marriage meant by scanning the lives of other people, we should know that something was seriously wrong.

These human analogies are standard, but after all they are not self-authenticating. Perhaps they are merely naive? For all their attractiveness, one might conceivably have to put them aside as leading into more difficulties than they are worth: in other words, it is no more than an assumption that God's chief contact with the world is in personal relationship. The "personalist" approach already stands in need of defence. It seems to lead at an early stage to a thoroughly subjective view of grace, to put the whole concept at the mercy of the individual believer's own conscious awareness.

Nor are the rival analogies for grace by any means dead which speak in terms of a power or substance imparted to men by God like petrol pumped into a motor car. At a superficial level such an impersonal model can certainly be attacked, on the ground that the ways of talking about God's grace to which it lends itself readily become pedestrian, mechanical and even commercial: but the terminology of relationships which the personalist happens to find more congenial can likewise be attacked, on the ground that the ways of talking about God's grace to which *it* lends itself readily become insipid, sentimental and even presumptuous. A sensitive exponent of either view can surely be careful to avoid such immediate pitfalls.

A theory in which one can intelligibly talk about God's grace operating in people whether they themselves recognise it or not clearly has something to recommend it. Grace on such a view is understood as something entirely specific, an actual force to be reckoned with, hard to identify perhaps but a matter of reality or unreality, there or not there as an objective fact whatever anyone thinks about it. Who would want to desert such a solid conception in favour of a merely relational understanding of grace?[1]

Yet to those reared, for example, on the personalism of Oman, the denigratory "merely" belongs to the idea that grace is a *thing*. "Not merely a thing *but* a relation" has seemed a thoroughly satisfactory formula in which to settle down, and it can be somewhat disconcerting to be uprooted. Yet on reflection it becomes clear that the reality of grace could be at stake here, and that it could be the personalist who is jeopardising it. It may even be facile to say that grace is not a thing but God's attitude of favour towards us: one must also insist that grace makes a difference to human beings, and this is most easily said in a terminology which makes grace itself something real, a substance or a specifiable attribute which people can "have". For example, if we say that a boy has a wicked uncle or that a car has a proud owner we have said something only indirectly about the boy or the car, but if we say that a boy is full of vigour or a car is full of petrol we have said something much more direct. Likewise we want to be able to say that people are full of grace, not only that God is looking favourably upon them.

The personalist of course will speedily reply that relationships need not be as "mere" as all that. For one thing, they can have effects which become extremely direct. A wicked uncle may smother his nephews in the Tower; a proud owner may run his car into a lamp post; the favour of God may receive us into Heaven. But more fundamentally, relations and attributes cannot in any case be so crisply distinguished from one another, for they run into each other. Is it an attribute or a relation of a piece of Roman masonry that the sun is shining gloriously upon it? Indeed if a non-personal model for God's grace is wanted one might well commend

[1] I owe the (to me) startling but enlightening conjunction of "merely", and "relational" to Mr. Anthony Kenny, in a paper read some years ago.

the model of sunshine as quite as promising as the model of petrol. It is as real as petrol but much less tangible; it has just as palpable results but cannot be handled, stored up, bargained over; its effects are much more various than the effects which petrol can have upon a machine; it can be gentle or relentless, a gleam or a blaze; and it has all the biblical overtones of light as opposed to darkness.

Perhaps it seems so attractive simply because it is not only already relational but also very nearly a personal analogy after all. At our end, we can talk about human beings responding to the light and heat of the sun in a fashion which is frankly personal not analogical at all; and at the divine end it is no far cry from the sun in the heavens to a pagan sun god or even to our God who makes the sun rise on the just and on the unjust. Sunshine indeed is an admirable picture of God's favourable (perhaps relentlessly favourable) attitude towards us, which is one aspect of God's grace which the "personal relationships" model was designed to bring out.

But of course it remains an impersonal model. To bask or to grow and flourish in the sunshine or even to move into it out of the shade is not to "enter into relationship" in the sense in which to become an uncle has potentialities of "entering into relationship". Essentially the weather cannot be "mindful" of us. Not only are there things we cannot say about God in this language: there are distorting things we shall be tempted to say if we press this illustration, this parable, into a full-scale analogy. We can hardly do justice to His concern for us if we insist on using impersonal images for it; but worse, we shall actually falsify, for instance, His impartiality. The weather is plainly not apportioned to our deserts: sun and rain fall not merely without respect of persons but indiscriminately upon the just and the unjust. If persisted in, this image would soon distort the sense in which God's grace is "not apportioned to our deserts". A Christian whose catchword is "personal relationship with God" will be anxious to point out, not that we deserve a different apportionment of grace but that "desert" and indeed "apportionment" simply are inept, almost irreverent, terms here.

"Relationship" after all is an ambiguous word. It can mean no more than "relative position" and if this were all we should surely not want to confine ourselves to "merely relational" terms in talking about the reality of God's grace. Even of "personal relationship" there are many kinds, and some of them can mean very much or very little. But those who take "relationship" as their favourite model have already, legitimately or illegitimately, filled it out in their own minds to mean something richly personal, at least as much on God's side as on ours. They are bound to feel that no impersonal language can do justice to the aspect of God's grace in which He is *kind* to the unthankful and evil.

It may well be said that such people are not looking for a model or illustration at all but trying, perhaps vainly, to speak literally about God. If someone believes that God *is* a Person or (more cautiously) that He *is* personal, then of course he will find that there are many things that cannot be said about Him except in fully personal language. Would it not be better simply to shed the pretence that he is only using a potentially fruitful parable and appear as an honest anthropomorphist? Is not the "personal relationships" model convincing because secretly it is not meant as a model at all but the plain truth? Maybe; but if the personalist wants to be cautious he still can be. He can propose to take human personal relationships as we know them for the most adequate and indeed best authorised model for the obscure relationship between man and God, committing himself only to the position that this model is not irrelevent nor irreverent, not to any precision about *how* good a model it may be, how plainly the divine nature can be characterised as "personal".

Certainly the personalist has every right to urge that when people say that grace is not an impersonal thing or force but is God Himself as He is known to us, they are apt to be at the beginning of fruitful discussion. He may well commend the constructiveness of Oman's way of posing the problem: "The way to understand the nature of grace is not to theorise about the operation of omnipotence, but to ask ourselves, What is a moral personality, and, how is it succoured?"[1]

Nor need we expect any one human description of the grace of God to be *the* correct and adequate view in the sense that its truth will render the rival views false: we are dealing in pictures not formulae. There is no reason why we should not take the advice of Professor Wisdom, in his discussion of the "Other Minds" problem, and deal toughly with our models.[2] If one is too simple, it may bring out the faults of another. We must not "stop at any of the comparisons on the way" but "keep control of the notations" and use them "at our convenience" to bring out the points we want. If this is good advice in sorting out epistemological problems about the mysteriousness of each other, it may well be good advice in sorting out epistemological problems about the mysteriousness of our relationship with God.

But the more the personalist defends his right to try his approach, the more inescapable becomes the empirical challenge. Can he pin down this "personal relationship with God" on which so much turns? If one is content to say, "God imparts His grace by many channels and it is not dependent upon our recognition of it" the challenge never becomes so acute; but if one takes one's stand upon relationship, in the last resort one will have to say something about the particular relationship which on this view ought to be most evidently real, one's own actual or potential acquaintanceship with God. If grace seems less tangible here than elsewhere can one put all the blame on one's own sinfulness or is the reality of grace at least a little impugned?

"If" it seems less tangible; well, does it or does it not? I shall be asked; and of course with due reticence and humility one sheers off the autobiographical. The central core of the problem of grace has very strong lines of defence, and one of them is this entirely proper

[1] *Grace and Personality*, p. 45, (Fontana, 1960).
[2] "Other Minds", pp. 200, 206 (Blackwells 1952). See below, p. 129.

reticence which makes one most reluctant to probe where grace presumably is to be found and see what one does find. One would much rather take refuge in what seems plain piety: of course we experience God's grace in our lives, if we claim to be Christians at all. But if the sceptical issue has been raised and we have to do battle there are still ways of choosing our own battleground and fighting over certain traditional outposts rather than over this sacred central territory itself.

For the core of the problem of grace, the point at which God is supposed to impinge upon the individual soul, is heavily overlaid by a proliferation of notorious overlapping difficulties some of which have a great deal of life in them. Notwithstanding their interest as separate questions I believe that really they are all manifestations of the basic unease about grace that I have tried to indicate; and that their own intrinsic urgency is liable to obscure the more fundamental issue. It surely looks as if one has indeed an insidious subconscious temptation to use these problems, so pressing in their own right, as a screen to save one from having to face the fundamental issue. One embarks upon them with courage, aware that if like Milton's devils one finds no end, "in wandering mazes lost", at least one will have drawn the enemy's fire away from the central citadel for the present.

Because these pressing problems about grace are important in their own right they cannot simply be ignored; but equally, they cannot be briefly solved and cleared out of the way. The most convenient compromise seems to be to try to disentangle them from one another and then place them as tidily as possible on one side, not solved but as it were packed up so that other matters can be attended to. They divide roughly into four: four familiar problems about grace, offering themselves as major problems but, I suggest, better regarded for the present as subsidiary problems. Of course they overlap, but still they seem distinct enough to be worth distinguishing. They are the problems of Providence (with Miracle as an extreme case); of Freedom; of Virtue; and of Fact.

The problem of Grace and Providence is concerned with the way in which God acts in the world. Can He, as it were, push His creatures about, and if He can, will He? Is His action confined to personal influence upon personal beings, or does He act as a kind of physical cause upon the material creation? May "law of nature" be defined in such a way as to make the concept of miracle logically possible and theologically significant?

The problem of Grace and Freedom posits divine grace as a gift to human beings and asks whether it does not make puppets of them. If God acts in or upon people, how can they be said to act for themselves? Theological determinism is traditionally as dangerous an enemy to freewill as scientific determinism. In relation to the mighty claims of causal law and divine grace human freedom is a kind of Lepidus, the "poor third" in an awkward triumvirate which can never be content to divide the universe up into three spheres of influence.

The problem of Grace and Virtue is the same problem seen from the point of view of moral responsibility. Is St. Paul's "not I, but the grace of God"[1] morally coherent? If I am not allowed to take any credit for my good actions, why must I still blame myself for my sins? Does the traditional distinction between "acquired" and "infused" virtue shed any light on these matters, or does it merely confuse the issue?[2] If certain virtues are gifts of God which cannot be acquired by human efforts, how can we have any duty to cultivate them? What steps are we supposed to take to encourage or allow God to bestow His grace upon us?

The problem of Grace and Fact is the problem of how the claim that God bestows His grace upon the world, once made, is to be substantiated. If there are alternative explanations, if after all our experience could perfectly well arrange itself in the way it does without the grace of God, does not the grace of God

[1] I Cor. 15: 10.
[2] This aspect of the question was raised rather sharply by Mr. McPherson in a paper on "Christian Values", *Proceedings of the Aristotelian Society*, Supplementary Volume (1963), XXXVII.

remain an unnecessary hypothesis? This I take it was the specific problem with which Professor Mitchell was concerned in his *Faith and Logic* article, and I am in no way trying to impugn his answer, or indeed any of the answers which have been put forward to any of these traditional thorny problems.[1]

The present question is whether the variegated answers we may feel disposed to give are or are not upheld by a basic and well-founded certainty about grace. If we have the necessary key idea of what it means to say that one is in a personal relationship with God, if we know for ourselves when we want to make these claims, the urgency of the particular problems is much diminished and there is much better hope that eventually they will become clearer. If not, we can make debating points about Providence, Freedom, Virtue and Fact indefinitely but will never fully convince ourselves or other people.

"If" we have the key idea: it will be noticed that I am still dealing in "ifs". But what I take to be the core of the problem has to be reached sooner or later and it is absolutely necessary to stop saying "If we have such and such a relationship with God" and start asking "Have we?" The small child will have to be heard if the Emperor is to have any peace. Unfortunately, even if we arrive at the point of trying with all our might to begin to be candid, it is by now almost too late for the answer to be an unequivocal "yes" or "no". For whether we are Christians or sceptics we have been conditioned so thoroughly to interpret our experience in the way we do interpret it that it has become almost impossible to see plainly what data we are basing our interpretation upon, what in fact our experience itself consists of.

There are two partial answers to be made here, and one of them has to be a blatant anticipation of a position which cannot be properly appreciated until much

---

[1] The first problem, of God's possible action in the physical world, is not the theme of this book, except in so far as Chapter II is relevant to it. How grace can avoid making puppets of us is touched upon in Chapter V; and the problem of "Grace and Virtue" is the subject of Chapter X.

later in the argument.[1] It is essential to acknowledge at this stage the immense amelioration of the problem offered by a passage in Austin Farrer's *The Glass of Vision*.[2] "Amelioration" is still for the present the right word, not "solution": one is by no means yet in a position to make Dr. Farrer's line of thought fully one's own; but it would be simply dishonest just to carry on with the argument as though Dr. Farrer had never written, producing his insight much later as if it were entirely new. It is fairer to put it in place here as an anticipation, hoping to do it more justice at a later stage. The passage deserves to be quoted at length:

I should now like to ask how important it is deemed to be that the philosopher's experience should fall into the form of an inward colloquy, with one part of his thought addressing another as though with the voice of God. I have a special and personal interest in challenging the colloquy-form, because of an obstacle I remember encountering in my own adolescence. I had myself (this at least is the impression I retain) been reared in a personalism which might satisfy the most ardent of Dr. Buber's disciples. I thought of myself as set over against deity as one man faces another across a table, except that God was invisible and indefinitely great. And I hoped that he would signify his presence to me by way of colloquy; but neither out of the scripture I read nor in the prayers I tried to make did any mental voice address me. I believe at that time anything would have satisfied me, but nothing came; no "other" stood beside me, no shadow of presence fell upon me. I owe my liberation from this *impasse*, as far as I can remember, to reading Spinoza's Ethics. Those phrases which now strike me as so flat and sinister, so ultimately atheistic, *Deus sive Natura* (God, or call it Nature), *Deus, quatenus consideratur ut constituens essentiam humanae mentis* (God, in so far as he is regarded as constituting the being of the human mind) – these phrases were to me light

[1] See below pp. 208–9.
[2] Dacre Press, 1948, pp. 7–8.

and liberation, not because I was or desired to be a pantheist, but because I could not find the wished-for colloquy with God.

Undoubtedly I misunderstood Spinoza, in somewhat the same fashion as (to quote a high example) St. Augustine misunderstood Plotinus, turning him to Christian uses. Here, anyhow, is what I took from Spinozism. I would no longer attempt, with the psalmist, "to set God before my face". I would see him as the underlying cause of my thinking, especially of those thoughts in which I tried to think of him. I would dare to hope that sometimes my thoughts would become diaphanous, so that there should be some perception of the divine cause shining through the created effect, as a deep pool, settling into a clear tranquillity, permits us to see the spring in the bottom of it from which its waters rise. I would dare to hope that through a second cause the First Cause might be felt, when the second cause in question was itself a spirit, made in the image of the divine Spirit, and perpetually welling up out of his creative act.

Such things, I say, I dared to hope for, and I will not say that my hope was in any way remarkably fulfilled, but I will say that by so viewing my attempted work of prayer, I was rid of the frustration which had baffled me before.

To the Christian trying to pray, this is inspiring; but of course the "small child" is still clamouring for something more definitely evidential, and an answer directly addressed to him will have to be attempted. The fairest thing for the Christian to say now is that his experience of what he takes to be the grace of God falls somewhere between the two limits of indubitable relationship and absolute blank: in other words, it consists of hints and hopes. Such a statement is vague enough to command agreement: it is therefore too vague to be much use. It is essential to specify further. Unfortunately we lack criteria for assessing the significance of these "hints and hopes", partly because both Christians and sceptics have a reluctance to admit the need for criteria at all. A sceptic has no wish to take these fancies seriously, and a Christian is distressed at the irreverence of seeming to ask God for His credentials; so Gigadibs calls the chessboard black and Blougram calls it white, and either way the real nature of our experience escapes enquiry.

Let us then try calling it chequered. This involves making the claim that we can pick out these hints and hopes; and here indeed we have at last found a claim which I should be willing to make. I do not think it is a very large claim, as it certainly does not rule out the possibility that hints and hopes may be self-induced; but let it anyway be said that they are not non-existent. There are moments, some primarily moral, some primarily aesthetic, when the concept of the holy seems to take on definite shape and one has a faint idea of what worship might be. However little one is prepared to build upon such moments, it would be a lie to say, "I have absolutely no religious experience".

Simply to make this tiny claim, or admission as it might rather be called, does little or nothing to answer the original question, not how to interpret such an experience once it has been specified, but how to set about discerning it at all, how to identify it as a topic for consideration. How indeed can we ever identify the presence of grace, since notoriously there should be nothing to contrast it with? The experience of God's apparent absence, though familiar enough to many people, does not supply a sufficiently clearcut contrast to the elusive, dim, maybe self-induced impression that after all He is there.

The problem is acute: yet it may now be slightly abated. There is a situation which one can more distinctly begin to contrast with the presence of God: not His absence, but the presence of a false God. One sometimes becomes aware that one has been making God in one's own image and praying habitually to an idol, an idol who can even be made to give answers but whose answers will always be the perpetual reflections of one's own thoughts. The unwelcome character of some of these answers does not ensure their objectivity: one can insult oneself, harangue oneself, blame oneself, deny oneself, and still hear no voice but one's own. To reject this idol may often involve falling back upon scepticism, but sometimes one seems fleetingly to be enabled to reject the idol in the name of a Being who really is Another, who requires one to stop putting words into His mouth, who has the unpredictable disconcerting quality of the God and Father of our Lord Jesus Christ, who directs one's attention away from oneself, who is relaxed where the idol is grim and immensely awe-inspiring where the idol is puny. There is no trick for getting in touch with this God, but just occasionally, and not at all according to merit, it seems as if a barrier had been removed. Who is to say that He is not another idol? At least He is a more subtle and convincing one.

This is all very tentative and indeed flimsy. There is no question of basing upon it any kind of "argument from religious experience". What it is meant to do is play the humbler but necessary role of counting against a potentially rather strong sceptical argument from the absence or practical inaccessibility of religious experience. If one can truthfully affirm even so little as this, one is not entirely unable to indicate when challenged what one means by grace as it impinges upon one's own life. But let it none the less be rated as low as possible. Let the chessboard be called black flecked with white. It becomes essential to go on to enquire whether if one starts with such a minimal understanding of grace it is possible to build upon it a doctrine which is recognisably Christian.

INCARNATIONAL DEISM

CHAPTER FOUR

What Think Ye of Christ?

Making positive statements about God's dealings with His creatures is not something to be done glibly. A rough sketch of the form these dealings might take assumed a somewhat pantheistic appearance;[1] but now it is time to look at deism, pantheism's much more cautious converse, in order not to lose touch with what the world really looks like. This chapter and the next two will be an excursion along a narrow path which might be signposted "Incarnational Deism". Although it may eventually lead into a cul-de-sac, it is a route which strikes conveniently through some difficult country at the outset. It is worth finding and pursuing it for as far as it will go.

Ordinary Deism is the idea that the good God made the world and then left it to its own devices; and this is evidently both theologically and scientifically discredited, for a Christian wants to say a great deal more and a scientist has no need of such an hypothesis. But, in reacting against this unsatisfactory view, a Christian tends to arrive at a very high doctrine of grace. He repudiates Deism completely, insisting that God must be positively active in every event in His world, even if the empirical facts appear to be recalcitrant. This is the point at which one begins to be dogged by all the difficulties I have tried to pick out. One can neither substantiate this anti-deistic view of divine activity, nor even say what it would be like to substantiate it. The various parcels into which the problem has been packed begin to come undone, and the various strands of Providence, Freedom, Virtue and Fact seem to be as tangled as ever.

For example, pick up the strand of Fact. At this stage

[1] See above, pp. 33–4, 51–2.

it is salutary to admit just how recalcitrant the empirical facts often are. It is not so much that they tell against a theory of divine grace as that they appear to be almost aggressively neutral. Say X is ill. Y prays for X, and X improves beyond expectation. Y thanks God; but owing to native caution or sinful doubt dares not feel utterly convinced that this is a specific example of an act of God. X cannot immediately get a hospital bed for treatment and deteriorates again. Y goes on praying in much confusion of mind. Of course one could assign a role to grace in this story in several ways, most of which would be variants on the theme "these things are sent to try us"; but is it not completely artificial to do anything of the sort? To acquire the vision that sees God in all things may indeed enlarge our understanding and deepen our sensitivity; but if we try to act on this vision are we not doing something like trying to sit down on Van Gogh's yellow chair?

Indeed to see the hand of God too pertinaciously in one's own concerns may not be to enlarge one's vision at all but to restrict it, to look on the Almighty as a "respecter of persons" in a thoroughly trivial way. A Christian remembers "providentially" that he is supposed to be at a meeting and rushes off just in time; but how can he presume to thank Providence for jogging his elbow when Providence has not said "Don't", perhaps the same day, to someone opening a car door as a child went by on a bicycle? It begins to seem more humble as well as more prudent for the Christian to admit that many things do just happen, and that it is pig-headed or even irreverent to try to trace God's hand in them in any very specific way.

This is the point at which one stops to ask, "What then is so very wrong with Deism from a Christian point of view?" The answer is at once obvious: "It leaves out the Gospel." Put in the Gospel then, and see how far this move can help. It is worth exploring the suggestion that it will help a great deal. For however little the individual Christian feels able to say about the activity of God in his own experience, he has after all something definite to point at to give his faith particular empirical reference.

"This", he can say, "the Incarnation, Death and Resurrection of Jesus Christ, is what I primarily mean by divine activity. Begin to see the point of saying that God was in Christ, and the idea of grace is grounded. The rest is superstructure." Having affirmed this, one is in a position to fit in whatever one feels driven to say about one's own individual relationship to God, be it overwhelming or vanishingly inconspicuous. A thoroughly incarnational religion can make room for either of these possibilities. But if one takes one's own religious experience as evidentially primary one will surely be thought to inhabit, and may very likely actually come to inhabit, a dream world, the world of the Emperor's New Clothes.

The movement of thought so far has been something like this. At the first stage one has some kind of concept of God, however arrived at, a God who in the Christian tradition is supposed to be both personal and immaterial. This concept sooner or later stands in need of defence against the charges of being incoherent or empty. I have tried to defend it against the first charge by attempting to show that an infinite person could be "immaterial" in a sense in which a finite person could not; or, to put it differently, that God the Creator could be said to stand in a kind of "bodily ownership" or "animating" relationship with the whole of matter, on which His particular dealings with physical beings could somehow be based.

But there is no point in saying any of this with such difficulty unless there is some reason to believe it true. Knowledge of God must somewhere become actual in human life, not constantly vanish over the horizon like the pot of gold at the rainbow's end. Hence the importance of one's own "hints and hopes". For most people they prove nothing positive, but by rebutting an otherwise forbidding negative they give one the right to start on a quest. Without them God's presence would always be somewhere else: jam yesterday and jam tomorrow but never jam today.

But in practice "hints and hopes" are apt to be elusive and even subjective, and God's grace is far from being publicly obvious. Rather than risking deceiving himself and others by making too much of inexorably scanty evidence, the Christian can take the world as it comes and make one definite objective affirmation: that to find the activity of God in the world the clearest place to look is the life of Jesus of Nazareth, the Incarnate Son. Explicitly to take this line is to become, anyway provisionally, an Incarnational Deist.

Of course to affirm the Incarnation is only to stake a claim. The theologian will have to elaborate it, the philosopher analyse it, the apologist try to substantiate it; but the trouble with so many Christian statements about the grace of God is that they seem to fail to make any specific claim at all. What is at issue is the viability of the very notion of God as a Being who makes some difference to the world.

If this viability is indeed manifested by the Incarnation, it must be in a fairly complex way. The complexity is worth unravelling a little in order to see what Incarnational Deism could amount to. To begin with we have as some kind of given fact the life and death of Jesus of Nazareth as seen by us through the eyes of some of his immediate followers. Forthwith one has to reckon with the further and this time indubitable fact that this particular life and death has been morally and religiously central for innumerable people since the first century. It does not instantly follow that these people have "identified the grace *of God*" for the purposes of the present argument. The currently fashionable way of characterising the significance of Christ does not say much about God's grace. It calls Jesus of Nazareth the "man for others" in that through his whole life, teaching and death he stood for the unique and ultimate value of self-giving love. Some of those who think in this fashion see it as an advantage that along this line one can call oneself a Christian, align oneself in loyalty beside this man, live in his spirit and find meaning in life through faith in him, without concerning oneself with a super-natural Deity at all. If grace does not come into the world from outside, there is no problem about identifying its arrival to which Incarnational Deism need be seen as an answer.

Pastorally, the relevance here of "he that is not against us is for us"[1] ought to be sufficiently obvious: Christians are forbidden to repudiate those who would wish to take the name of Christ upon them. But intellectually they are still at liberty to point out that such a non-supernatural Christology is unstable, in at least two ways. For one thing, it is paradoxical to deny supernaturalism while giving one's whole-hearted allegiance to a leader who, if anything is clear about him at all, taught that whole-hearted allegiance belongs to God. For another, it has never been made clear why if human self-giving love is the only ultimate, Jesus Christ should be given such a unique regard for exemplifying it. Other men have lived more obviously for others, and faced even greater sufferings. To put one's faith in him simply as *the* man for others looks like living on theological capital: it is because one is used to thinking of him as God incarnate coming to this world to live and die in it for all men that one is so struck by his self-giving love as to be constrained to call it divine.

Put like that, the circle is obvious. Unfortunately the argument seems to cut both ways: if the radical Christian cannot know Christ is divine without knowing he is God, how can the traditional Christian know he is God without knowing already that he is divine? It is tempting to say that for evidences of the Incarnation as for evidences of grace in my own life, I have to find what I am looking for before I can expect to find it. But this would be to over-simplify. The incarnational argument is more subtle than a straightforward but question-begging move from Christ's goodness to his Godhead. The uniqueness of Christ is not established, only supported, by the evidence for his holiness. Many men have gone down to history as holy men. What seems to stand out about Jesus Christ is the peculiar and even paradoxical relationship between a specific kind of holiness which sets store by meekness and humility, and an equally characteristic quality which might be called authoritativeness. Whether or not he claimed explicitly to be the Son of God, he seems to have comported himself in a way

[1] Mark 9: 40.

which is only consistent with his own teaching on the
assumption that he was more than just a struggling
fellow-sufferer and sinner. "*Aut deus, aut homo non bonus.*"
He showed his followers the way of repentance but unlike
Isaiah or Peter or Paul he did not tread it himself.

The incarnational argument sets out first to establish
this curious interplay between the character of Christ
and his authoritativeness, so posing not solving the
problem, What think ye of Christ? For the vindicating
and welding together of this character and this authoritativeness into the *authority* of Christ a further step is
indispensable: the announcement of the Resurrection.
If the Cross is the end of the story, the life and death of
Jesus, however morally attractive, are simply no answer
to the troubles of the world. To quote the text "If Christ
be not raised your faith is vain"[1] is not just to make a
debating point, though it ought to be to state the obvious.

If the authority of Christ cannot be established,
Christianity falls apart into a miscellaneous set of ideals.
If it can, then the grace of God can properly be located
in his Incarnation. The evidence for establishing it
must be found in an intricate network of fact and value
judgment which a full apologetic would need to sort out.
Such an apologetic would be a matter of giving reasons
for trusting the veracity and judgment of a group of men
in the first century about the occurrence and significance
of certain events. "But then", it will be said, "you are
putting the Christian faith at the mercy of historians,
critics and archaeologists." So be it. If it can be shown
that, for instance, the wrong man died on the cross,
then I cannot call myself a Christian any more. I shall
probably be rather sceptical of recurring attempts to
show this, so I can be blamed for wishful thinking or
praised for tenacious faith, but the psychology of believers
does not swallow up the logic of belief.

There is a tendency to forget that even if one demytholo-
gises and takes a minimal view of what in fact happened
at the first Easter, there still has to be a history. Jesus
died and was buried, and then what? People came
somehow to hold certain beliefs about him, which they

[1] 1 Cor. 15: 17.

expressed in certain specific ways, and which are still offered to the world for acceptance or rejection. If practically all their specific statements are to be characterised as myth rather than literal truth their reliability becomes so Pickwickian as to give their would-be successors remarkably little standing ground. People say in scorn, "But does your Christianity depend upon the Empty Tomb?" In this they commit the fallacy of Many Questions. To the question, "Could you believe in a Christ who revealed his victory over death in some less crude way?" the answer is, "Maybe: it depends on the revelation". To the question, "Can you believe in Christ on the word of men whose basic message about him *cannot* be believed in anything like the literal sense in which they believed it?" the answer must be, "I hardly can".[1]

But am I hereby committed to swallowing the Bible whole? A similar argument to the present one is used by fundamentalists about the Old Testament: if the compiler of the Pentateuch is mistaken in his own terms or misleading in ours concerning the origin of the universe how can I put my faith in him concerning the nature of God?[2] The answer is that in fact I do not put my faith in the Pentateuch concerning the nature of God. I put my faith in Christ by way of the credibility of the early Christians about events in their own time. So, as a result of Christian belief, not as a ground of it, I find myself able to stand in the Mosaic religious tradition in which Christ and his apostles were educated and which they did not repudiate. This approach allows for the recognition that the remoter origins of the Hebrew religion are wrapped in myth and legend. The non-arrival of the expected Second Coming remains an apologetic problem;[3]

---

[1] I realise that many biblical scholars would deny that the "basic message" involved an Empty Tomb. I have discussed the physical character of the Resurrection a little further in an article in *Theology* (March 1967), from which some paragraphs in this chapter are taken. See John Baker, *The Foolishness of God*, pp. 263, 267, (Darton, Longman & Todd, 1970).

[2] For reminding me of the likelihood of this criticism I am indebted to Dr. D. D. Evans.

[3] Though for the present writer appreciably less of one since John Baker's *The Foolishness of God*.

the non-historical character of the Book of Genesis does not.

To discuss the Resurrection in terms such as these is not merely to trespass on the historian's province, as if one were to discuss (say) why Brutus killed Caesar. What needs to be undertaken is a twofold enterprise: to make sense of the theology and to do justice to the evidence. What needs to be resisted is the attempt to prise these apart. Neither can stand on its own feet, but there seems no reason why either should be expected to.

On the one hand, the enterprise of making sense of the theology requires attention to the evidence. A theology not grounded in something which can respectably be called fact remains abstract and indeed unreal. On the other hand, the enterprise of doing justice to the evidence requires attention to the proposed theology. Alleged facts of a miraculous nature remain frankly incredible, as Hume insisted, unless one's mind is at least open to a theological interpretation adequate to bear their weight. The argument is not just that these matters must be determined by one's presuppositions which one has presumably arrived at by some sort of existentialist leap. It is rather that the interplay between empirical interpretation and theological understanding of the data is closer and more complex than any severance between the two enterprises will allow.

To put it crudely: one can swallow a miracle, take it into one's conceptual scheme, if it is *both* well supported by evidence *and* set in a framework of strong coherent theology. It is not merely that each of these gives a weak support which put together can just bear the weight. It is rather that either *kind* of support is weak alone but that the combination of them can be strong. There is no need to contradict Hume in saying this. A miracle cannot be proved so as to be the foundation of a system of religion: fair enough. To believe in a miracle requires such an upheaval in one's empirical conceptual framework as to impair the stability of one's whole empirical understanding: better then to reject *one* set of evidences however plausible. (For instance, if an ordinary mortal claims to have risen from the dead, it is more rational to think him mistaken or fraudulent, more rational to look for a scientific explanation, more rational even to think "I am going mad", than to worship him as a new Christ.) To modify one's conceptual framework itself in such a way as not to impair its stability requires more than empirical data. It requires surely the kind of complex combination of fact and theology which the New Testament accounts of the Resurrection purport to supply.

Any Christian who is not prepared to stake everything on the inescapability of his own religious experience must either conduct some such historical and theological enterprise for himself or depend upon the fact that other people can conduct it. If he cannot simply say to himself or others, "Well, look and see", and if he is not willing to make a totally arbitrary choice, he stands in need of an apologetic, a reason for the faith that is in him. To ignore or belittle the relevance of the Resurrection claim to belief in Christ may be to evade the question of what such belief in effect amounts to.

If anyone finds himself able to accept the divine authority of Christ as based upon some such interplay of history and theology as I have tried to suggest, he has a point of contact between God's grace and the world.[1] If God's nature has been so revealed, one is claiming something real and specific when one tries through prayer, sacrament or Bible to enter into relationship with Him. One need not be dependent upon any spiritual success of one's own. The empirical facts of the world can indeed be accepted whatever they may turn out to be, without divine Providence running the gauntlet of the "death by a thousand qualifications". A Christian may be much more deistic in his daily life than traditional Christianity has been, without impugning the fundamental relevance of divine activity to human affairs.

This Incarnational Deism is in no way concerned to minimise the grace of God where the facts seem to suggest it. It leaves it entirely open to a Christian to posit the grace of God as an explanation in the kind of

[1] The case is strikingly put by David Jenkins in *The Glory of Man*, (S.C.M., 1967). See especially pp. 22f. and 31f.

situation to which Professor Mitchell has drawn attention;[1] as for example when one is confronted by the kind of holiness which seems to transcend the purely natural and stretch into a supernatural dimension. But this way of thinking avoids the necessity of trying to make room forcibly for grace where it does not seem to fit.

So far Incarnational Deism may sound a somewhat dreary and faint-hearted theory of grace. "Make the smallest claim you can", it seems to say, "and perhaps some of the difficulties will never arise." This is needlessly negative: the Christian Gospel is not a small claim. To pin one's faith to the belief that one has been bought with a price is far more exhilarating than to pin one's faith to a benevolent but obscure providence watching over one's affairs. A God who loves the unlovable and has been prepared to have that love put to the test is a more completely satisfying object of worship than the most elaborately conceived tutelary spirit. To lay stress on the Incarnation as the paradigm case of divine activity is by no means to make God remote or unreal. Far from minimising grace, it focuses it, it gives the concept specific reference.

It will inevitably be objected that this line of thought leads to a very low view of our personal relationship with God; but it now needs to be shown that this criticism is mistaken. Indeed, far from belittling personalism, Incarnational Deism lends itself surprisingly well to a strongly personalistic, even anthropomorphic, understanding of the relationship between God and human beings. This is because it has given its answer, for better or worse, to the positivist demand that Christian statements must submit to the test of "falsifiability". The Incarnational Deist, challenged to say how things would be different were there no God, does not have to stake everything on the assertion that there is a special providence in the fall of a particular sparrow, for it is in the Incarnation that his theology runs the gauntlet of falsifiability. He is therefore released from the incessant

[1] See above, p. 41–2.

pressure to find peculiar senses for words like "providence", "divine intervention", "fatherly care" when the facts do not appear to allow their more literal use. Maybe he will apply these personal concepts less frequently to the Almighty than some Christians do, but he will be able to apply them less equivocally. His parents have provided, intervened, cared for him by giving him bread not a stone; likewise God has provided, intervened, cared for him by dying on his behalf. If at present he happens to be starving in a garret or suffering from toothache, he must indeed believe that this is within God's ultimate purpose, but he does not have to contort himself to maintain that this is precisely what he means by God's loving concern.

The Incarnational Deist cannot presume to shake off the problem of evil, but for him its burden will be differently distributed. The strain will be placed upon his apologetic, not upon his daily Christian life. His faith will not be shaken by this or that example of misfortune which divine providence has not averted; but he will always be confronted by the question of whether such a world as this can have been created by a God at all. His doubt will always be fundamental doubt, of the substance not the details of the Christian faith. He feels the onus of proof lie heavily upon him, seeing the world as he does as a muddle of pleasure and pain, not at all as a web of providences. He must see that all this is or can become worthwhile before he can believe in the God who made it or worship Him as Creator. Two necessary claims are made on behalf of the Christian God: that He deemed it sufficiently worthwhile to enter in and bear the brunt in the person of His Son; and that at last He will consummate all things in Christ.[1] Without an Incarnation and a real Heaven, the world is too messy to give a foundation for belief in God. For this way of thinking, the alternative to Christianity is atheism, not some other kind of theology.

The upshot of these assertions comes somewhere between the tautology that all Christian Deists must be

---

[1] I have discussed this theme a little in an article called "Christian Flourishing", *Religious Studies*, vol. V (1969).

Christians, and the paradox that all Deists must be Christians or atheists. To put it less provokingly, the point is that the Incarnational Deist will tend to be unappreciative of, or even bored by, natural theology. He need not repudiate or deprecate the traditional arguments for belief in God apart from Christ, but they are hardly likely to come to life for him. They yield him no "cosmic disclosures", in Dr. I. T. Ramsey's phrase: they are pieces of dead philosophy, anatomical specimens.

What convinces him is the account of the Father who sent His Son; and so he begins in a thoroughly personalistic way. He is better, not worse placed, for saying what people want to say when they lay great stress on a personal relationship with God. For if he takes his stand on the kind of personal character God has shown Himself to have, rather than on any assumptions about what our experience of Him in everyday life is likely to turn out to be, he is in a position to insist that the relationship is fully real on God's side, however inadequate it may be on ours. Our inadequacy need not be reflected back upon God. There is no need to claim to be able to see the Emperor's new clothes, or to try to force God's grace into a mould of human devising. Instead one can say: "I believe, for such-and-such reasons, that He is there, and that His character is as Christ revealed." In so far as I enter into relationship with Him, in this world or the next, I am claiming something which is real already. For the present, subjective awareness of this real relationship is a luxury which I may or may not be granted. What matters is the fact, if fact it be, of what God is like. The Christian affirmation is that we have good reason to believe that He is indeed a fully personal Being whose nature is unwavering holy love. This is something to be held to and acted upon.

The language of such an affirmation has an old-fashioned ring about it today, with its "God out there", whose character is a "fact" and whose Heaven is a plain future prospect. It will presently need to be qualified; though not entirely repudiated. Meanwhile its possibilities have not yet been sufficiently explored. The Incarnational Deist has more to say for himself before bowing himself out.

CHAPTER FIVE

A Preliminary Personalism

The moral possibilities of Incarnational Deism are very considerable; for once one has located God's grace decisively in the life, death and resurrection of Christ one is set free to think in fully personal terms of what He has done and what one owes to Him, and so to make use of all the insights which a personal rather than a legal morality promises to yield. God's love is not something too peculiar to be talked about but showed itself humanly. Therefore one has the right at least to begin anthropomorphically and consider the moral implications of the idea of God as personal, even for the time being as "a person", a real person with His own consciousness, character and purposes. I believe that it is to this conception that the intractable problems of duty and merit, law and love actually do begin to yield.[1] How does one try to please a person, to express one's love for him? – neither by fussy legalism nor by woolly permissiveness, but by coming unselfconsciously to want what he wants. Considerations about deserving his favour are gladly left behind, not roughly repudiated.[2] In response arising

[1] I have tried to show how in *Law and Love* (Faith Press, 1962) and *The Character of Christian Morality* (Faith Press, 1965).

[2] In making this point I am indebted to Mr. John Lucas who in an unpublished paper has set out a personalist ethic very clearly and has kindly given me permission to quote. He explains that "when we say that salvation cannot be earned, or that we are all miserable sinners, this is not to say that God is being less fair than Pelagius would have been, or that our customary moral distinctions are all invalid, but is, rather, an obscure way of saying that justice, which we do indeed deserve, is not what we want. What one can oblige another to do will never satisfy the heart's desire. What comes of right is not that worth having, and what is ultimately worth-while therefore can never be merited. When men do receive what is worth having they are often therefore overwhelmed with a sense of their being unworthy of it."
See also: Mr. Lucas's chapter in *Faith and Logic* on "The Soul", p. 147.

[continued overleaf]

out of relationship one can come to achieve what could never have been realistically or even fairly demanded of one.

This is personalism, certainly: but already it seems to have come a long way from deism. Surely "relationship with God" is precisely the concept the deist repudiates? The real point at issue might easily get lost here. It is not, of course, particularly deist to emphasise response rather than obedience. What is characteristic of the "Incarnational Deist" is to found such a personal morality, not upon day-to-day relationship with God, but upon what we believe to be the character of God as shown in the Gospels. He puts his faith in a living person, a person "out there" indeed, even a person apparently absent; and hopes to lead his own life in such a way as one day to get to know that person better, maybe at last to have it said "Well done, good and faithful servant". Meantime he is not anxiously watching for little tokens of favour or the reverse to crop up in his daily life, and at least in theory is quite prepared for the world around him to be relentlessly secular.

But how, it may well be asked, does such a Christian pray? And if he does not, is he not cutting himself off too decisively from the mainstream of tradition to call himself a real Christian at all? To this he has a positive though limited answer. First, he can align himself with some wise words of Kirk's:[1]

There are very many Christians who, without deprecating "mystical experience", shrink from claiming it for themselves, because it seems something too high for them. They shrink even from looking for it, lest – falling into some emotional self-hallucination – they mistake the false for the true. The impulses are laudable and salutary, though religion would be a colder thing than it is if it had nothing more to offer. But at least St. Paul[2] sets us on a safe road when he insists that

---

C. S. Lewis' picture in his volume in the *Oxford History of English Literature* of "What it felt like to be an early Protestant" further illuminates the same point, *English Literature in the Sixteenth Century*, p. 32ff, (Oxford, 1954).

[1] *Vision of God*, p. 105 (Longmans, second edition, 1932).

[2] He has just quoted I Cor. 8: 2.

in "seeing God" – whatever that phrase may mean in its fulness – the emotional experience here and now is secondary, and is never to be made the final test of genuine Christianity. What *matters* is that a man should have the right attitude – should love God and his neighbour. If he preserves this attitude, he may rest assured that (however much he doubts whether he "knows" God) he himself is "known" by God with a knowledge in which love, and providence, and the desire to give all that can be given, are equally compounded.

Secondly, let it be understood that Incarnational Deism is essentially an elementary approach to Christianity. Granted this, it has at this level something definitive, not negative, to say, at least about petitionary prayer, which is where the deist shoe pinches most. It cannot aspire fully to satisfy the wise but it may fulfil the role of an encouraging and not invalid introduction.[1]

One may begin with the strong and primitive human instinct to pray: to find a Lord and call upon his name. One finds this instinct backed up by the most elaborate and diverse arrangements and organisations encouraging people to pray, yet impugned from at least two directions: the "Emperor's New Clothes" attack, which insists that the evidence that prayer is heard is quite inadequate to support all this; and the more moralising line which suggests that "ask and get" offers an unworthy picture of both God and man.

The first of these attacks, if not atheist, is precisely deist. If one is attracted to deism it is no doubt at least partly because of this very argument. It is therefore tempting to succumb to both attacks, allowing the second to provide a kind of moral rationale for giving up the struggle to answer the first. But the *Incarnational* Deist is not at liberty to take this course, for he is committed to take full cognisance of the New Testament, and here to the surprise and maybe dismay of the sophisticated he finds strong support for the primitive "ask and get"

[1] I have discussed petitionary prayer in an article in *Theology* (February 1970).

approach. "Ask and ye shall receive" is not an isolated
text but a summary of a whole strand in the tradition.

As a deist he is only going to be able to give a partial
answer: essentially deism cannot explain positively how
God acts in the world. But he is not committed to maintain that his partial answer is all the answer there can
be, only that he may legitimately begin with it. He is
not, so to speak, anti-providence. It is just that he
acknowledges a greater degree of agnosticism about
providence than has been traditional among Christians.
His position is that provided he has grounds for belief
that God acted *once*, in Christ, no other particular proposed
instance of divine activity is indispensable; though
indeed if there were no other instances whatsoever
that seemed at all convincing, his belief in his one instance
would be weakened to vanishing point.

Granted that he can neither rule out God's activity
in the everyday world, nor readily find definite examples
of it, nor explain what it could be, how can he still
align himself with the Christian tradition of prayer?
He can do it by refusing to accept the second attack,
the moralising one, upon the instinct to ask God for
things, and taking his stand upon an explicitly personalistic
view.

For example he may take issue at this point with
Dr. J. A. T. Robinson who in a newspaper article
published not long after *Honest to God* repudiated the
human instinct to call upon God at moments of crisis or
alarm, characterising it as pandering to emotional
immaturity. In taking off in an aeroplane, Dr. Robinson
contended, a Christian "*ought* to be a practical atheist"
not "indulge in additional 'cover' " by praying in
the gap. Granted that such a prayer may be almost
entirely superstition, does not the renouncing of it
depersonalise God in a way quite foreign to the teaching
of Christ? Panic and fret crave childishly for the impossible miraculous intervention, and must be denied it:
this is true. But if it is "emotionally immature" to seek
the presence and support of other people when under-
going stress, then one would need to say that Christ
was thus immature at Gethsemane. It is not only children

who cling, literally or metaphorically, to people they trust when a crisis has to be faced, when encouragement is as constructive as intervention. To refuse to let God count as someone to be trusted in this sense is to impoverish one's theology, not to mature it. One can preach many sermons to oneself, as one loosens one's safety belt presently with relief, at the condescension of a God who is willing to be present at such a puny crisis, at the quality of relationship which has been manifested on His side and on one's own; but surely to deny or check the manifestation is to deny or repudiate the relationship, certainly not to advance from it.

"Has been manifested": again the personalist has carried away the deist, or at least the deist must stop and qualify. He is again admitting to a conviction that all his deeds and thoughts are open to God's view, and that on God's part the personal relationship is alive and perfect. But he is not basing this conviction upon experiences of his own which could be easily characterised as subjective, but upon his understanding of God's promises of old. It is a case of his human need for God's presence being allowed to express itself unchecked because he is able to believe intellectually that God is indeed present and concerned for him, however little he is actually conscious of such presence. If it should please God sometimes to give him a hint[1] or sign that he really is not alone in his need, he will be seized with an awe and gratitude much greater than if he had, so to speak, had the Almighty at the end of an internal telephone all along. He will be like a child at a birthday party whose present exceeds his hopes: perhaps like a child at the entrance of the Kingdom of Heaven.

But, one hopes, life does not consist entirely of special occasions and crises, and it would be a very shallow Christian whose prayer was entirely upon such an emergency footing. The Incarnational Deist who wants to call himself a Christian cannot merely jettison the idea of walking with God from day to day. He cannot afford to ignore the personalist insistence that God is concerned with the whole of our lives not just with

[1] See above, p. 52f.

special "religious" aspects of them: that if His love for us is to be taken seriously He must be interested in our happiness and welfare as well as in our virtue and piety. In particular, His will must be relevant to all our choices: they cannot be sorted out into matters of duty and matters of indifference, as if we were servants with an exacting job but some free time.

The Incarnational Deist will see the point of these affirmations, rooted as they are in various New Testament emphases.[1] At the same time he will be particularly aware of the difficulties both empirical and moral of postulating a day-to-day relationship with God on this basis. He is not able to brush aside the daunting question of whether God is really "interested in our welfare" in the sense such day-to-day influence presupposes; a deistic question which takes two forms, a Christian and a sceptical one. First, without necessarily doubting the existence of God we may well ask whether God's aims for us are sufficiently like our own aims to give us any right to expect divine assistance in our human problems. Perhaps to God all human choices *are* "indifferent", not in the sense that there are areas of our life with which God is unconcerned, but in the sense that all the things that please or worry or annoy us are in His eyes just raw material for the formation of our characters. If it is choice that matters, God will hardly interfere in our use of it. To argue that because He loves us He will guide us is as if a child were to say, "Of course Daddy will help with my homework. After all, he wants me to do well at school."

The sceptical argument is a positivistic development of the Christian one. The child comes to see why his father never actually helps with his homework partly because he never has the slightest reason to doubt that his father wants him to do well at school. But suppose his father never shows any noticeable reactions to his progress, never discusses his work with him, never makes any comment on his teacher's reports, and perhaps leaves him at a boarding school the whole term without writing any letters. The masters say, "This *will* please your father", but nothing ever seems to happen as a result,

[1] Especially in the Sermon on the Mount and the First Epistle of John.

and even the schools fees are paid anonymously by the bank. Yet the boy still writes to his father asking for advice about his future. Is this a good analogy for a Christian's prayers for guidance? If it is, what right has the plain believer to affirm that God is indeed "concerned with his welfare" in *any* sense?

The Incarnational Deist of all people will be unable to make use of the standard answer here, that God is quite different from another human being. On the contrary, to him this is really the problem. When he puts the problem in its Christian form and is told in reply that what would be interference with our free choice from a fellow creature is not interference from God because He is not an "other mind" acting on us from outside but is within us as well as around us, he will protest that this only darkens counsel. The guidance of our friends perhaps does not harm our freedom of choice *because* they are finite and external to us. We know their advice may be bad and we are not after all obliged to take it. But if God acts in us how can we keep any liberty of choice, however much we may talk about "perfect freedom"? As for the sceptical formulation of the problem, the proposed cure again only worsens the disease. If God is really closer to us than breathing how can we ever know that we are not just idealising our own breathing when we like to think we are listening to Him?

It is not that the Incarnational Deist particularly wants to attack the concept of divine immanence as such, or even to deny that eventually it will need to be brought in to supplement his own; but he is rightly insisting that at this stage it is still premature and unhelpful. It is a misuse of mystery to bring it in as an expedient when our intellectual difficulties get out of hand. The only satisfactory way to introduce theological categories is to be pushed on by the force of one's own argument or experience to find that they are the only ones that seem at all adequate; just as, to use a favourite apologetic example, the early Church arrived at the doctrine of the Trinity. To bring in paradoxical talk at too early a stage is, with apologies to Dr. I. T. Ramsey, to try to get the chocolate out of the machine before the penny has dropped.

Meantime the hopeful course for the Incarnational Deist is once more to go back to personalism, to continue to take seriously the idea of God as an Other Person, and to try to illuminate or at least clarify the idea of relationship with God by considering human relationships. What do we ask for when we ask other people for guidance? There are two extreme cases where the analogy is quite straightforward to apply. On the one hand we may simply want to be agreed with. We know what we propose to do but want someone to back us up, and if we get contrary advice we shall probably be annoyed. To try to make use of God in this way may be blasphemous, but it is not different in kind, only in degree, from trying to make use of our friends and relations in this way.

At the other extreme, far from having made up our minds already we may be unwilling to make them up at all. In asking for guidance we simply want to be told what to do and to be absolved from responsibility. To make oneself a doormat like this is certainly to jeopardise one's freedom of choice, but there is no theological or philosophical difficulty about it, for we have no reason to suppose that God ever indulges our wish for this kind of guidance. Oracles are notoriously ambiguous, but before the sceptical positivist can torment the theologian about this the personalist can supply them both with good reason why it should be so.

Again, in asking for guidance some people only want a chance to think aloud. They can set out their ideas better if they feel they have a friendly listener, and make their final decisions with a much clearer mind. Still no philosophical problem arises, although maybe a moral one does when their friends feel hurt at having no chance to give their opinions after all. God has infinitely more reason to be "hurt" if His people want only to ventilate their own ideas and never to receive a reply; but if He keeps his own counsel the positivist still has nothing to object to.

The difficulties start of course, as one would expect,

in the application of the analogy in the cases where it is genuine help in making choices which is wanted, not just approval or instructions or a chance to talk. Each of the so-to-speak sham examples of "asking for guidance" which has just been given is a sort of caricature of a real example, of a way in which people ask, and often receive, help from one another. The Incarnational Deist is alert to the possibility that, far from the difficulties being insuperable, these human ways of helping are indeed the most promising analogies for that "relationship to God" which he finds it needful as a Christian, but far from easy, to postulate. If he is to pursue this line he will certainly have to take a searching look at the different cases.

The most instantly attractive possibility relates to the third example, where someone is helped by a chance to think aloud. Fairly recently it has even become a norm for guidance, that people should be encouraged to make their own decisions with a friendly listener who never interferes: counselling, in the sense of non-directive counselling, is now a "good work" of the first importance. No longer do the wise conceive it as their duty to tell other people what to do: rather they are to show that they care by being good listeners and letting people work out their own salvation. How promising then to apply this concept to divine guidance, which is often only too obviously non-directive.

The analogy is a good one, and goes a long way; but only when it does not claim to go all the way. It can at least set one free from some unsatisfactory "pipeline to God" views. One learns to be grateful to the human adviser who instead of giving one a ready-made answer makes one think for oneself; one appreciates the authority-figure who expresses no judgment but listens and accepts; and so one comes to understand, as an explanation of God's well-kept silence, that if He intervened He would be less god-like not more. But one cannot go on for ever being grateful for silence. A good listener is not one who we begin to think has gone quietly away. The reason why non-directive counselling has seized many people's imagination as a kind of revelation is that it has come as a welcome or salutary contrast to the familiar kind of advice-giving which turns out to be cramping or patronising. But if non-directive counselling could drive out this other kind entirely it would not itself prove fully adequate. There comes a time in human consultations when it is not unreasonable to ask for something more, when people become aware that they can contribute more to one another than unjudging, undemanding acceptance. This time should come sooner, not later, when God is the helper. A major reason why human counsel should often, perhaps usually, be non-directive is that human judgment is fallible and indeed corrupt. The counsellor therefore learns to withhold it as an unworthy offering. But where we are concerned with God, surely it is we who should be good listeners rather than He?

The "counselling" model accordingly needs supplementing. Its incompleteness forces one to react in the opposite direction, and look now at the most sought-after but not very encouraging analogy for divine guidance: the asking and receiving of genuine advice from someone qualified to give it, of which the uncritical following of instructions, "making oneself a doormat", is the extreme case and caricature. Three very usual kinds come to mind. First, I have a problem in which I need expert advice, so I go to a doctor, an architect, or a solicitor, set out the facts, and let him interpret them and advise accordingly. Secondly, I want help from a maturer mind, so I take my difficulty to somebody of an older generation, somebody who has been through this kind of problem already, or somebody I respect as wiser than myself. Thirdly, I simply want an objective judgment, so I go to a friend who may not be older or wiser, but who can see the problem from outside instead of being closely involved in it. The three kinds may overlap. Do people consult priests as religious experts or as mature minds? – or child guidance counsellors for their experience or their objectivity? What characterises them all is that a specific service is being sought and rendered. The person whose advice is sought is not just a lay figure who remains passive, but contributes something definite.

The question is, would God be an ideal adviser in this sense, and if not, has one any right to go on talking of Him as personal? Superficially it would seem obvious that God must be the greatest of all experts, the most mature of all minds, and the most objective in the sense of being no respecter of persons; but the very concept of an "ideal adviser" is beset with difficulties as soon as the advice is expected to have a specific content. An honest human counsellor will give all the help he can. The good barrister puts his entire knowledge of the law at my disposal so far as it is relevant to my case, the sage will hold back nothing of his accumulated wisdom, the impartial friend will go into the whole question in the utmost detail. The limits of their help are the limits of their capacity. It is true that the parent may refuse help with homework, and at first sight this seems a promising analogy for our heavenly Father's refusal of divine assistance; but the reason why the parent refuses is that he is the wrong person to give it. If he were the best available teacher both in knowledge and skill at imparting it he would not hand over his child to somebody less able, nor say, "You must do it all yourself". It is true too that the teacher himself in fulfilling his proper role may refuse to give mechanical short-term help, but this is a matter of technique. Fundamentally his aim is to pass on to his pupil what he knows, and the limit, the point where the pupil finally "stands on his own feet", comes not where his teacher arbitrarily refuses to teach him any more but when he has learnt what that teacher has to teach.

But now suppose all these people rolled into one Wise Being, always at one's side. There is no need to be extravagantly existentialist to perceive that although human help of this kind is entirely legitimate, to be able to tap God's unlimited resources like this would in some curious way be cheating. It is not necessary, it is true, to go so far as to say that all freedom of choice would be taken away. People could still presumably have moral struggles against temptation and they could still exercise some personal tastes and preferences; but a whole range of their characters would be impoverished and large aspects of their present lives would become a sort of sham. The existentialist and the traditional headmaster meet here to insist that the way in which people confront problems and difficulties, not necessarily specifically moral ones, is the chief way in which personal character, whatever that is worth, is built up.

It begins to look as if the kind of human help we are used to is good for us only because of its inevitable limitations, and that if it were unrestricted it would pauperise us. Human advisers are not expected to be so "non-directive" as to withhold specific information; on the contrary, their role is to amass it and pass it on. They may desist from judging but they are allowed and expected to make recommendations about how best to achieve certain ends, or what the results of certain courses of action will be. But they are never omniscient nor perfectly wise. The idea of friends, parents, or professional advisers holding back help they could give is abhorrent, but they have no need to. Human guidance is something one can exhaust. We may look on this fact as a merciful dispensation of providence to allow people to stand sooner or later on their own feet; but this is at the heavy price of introducing a great difficulty into the concept of God. How can we imagine a perfectly wise, perfectly loving Being giving partial help like a lazy professional man? Where does He draw the line? Does not this way of thinking make the universe into rather an irritating game with artificially fixed rules? Or else, does it not make nonsense of all human values? Whatever people think they are trying to do, rule nations, write books, create beautiful objects, bring up children, enjoy themselves, God is never really on their side. All He is really interested in is character formation and to suppose Him to be directly interested in any worldly states of affairs is to deceive oneself. Human beings cannot help being interested in choosing effectively and getting answers: He only wants them to choose well and build up their personalities. This is the price of saying that there is a God who really knows best. If He gives people His help He pauperises them; if He rations it out the whole situation becomes artificial;

if He withholds it He is really playing quite a different game from them.

To make matters worse, at this point the sceptical difficulty about how God can ever be known becomes acute again. If we say that God is not potentially an ideal adviser in human problems the positivist will assuredly ask what is the use of postulating a God at all. If He is not the sort of being to take a hand in this world's affairs what sense does it make to say that statements about Him have any meaning for us? This is the way towards the death by a thousand qualifications.[1] But if we decide to be anthropomorphic and speak of God as a Father in Heaven who is both loving and efficient, the positivist has an even quicker attack: if He can advise, then why doesn't he? If theoretically there ought to be divine guidance, why is it so difficult to find empirically? After all, we really know perfectly well that God does not pauperise us; but how do we manage to be so uncertain about the other alternatives? Is it not extremely curious, the positivist will argue, that claiming as we do to be Christians living in a loving personal relationship with God we cannot simply cut through this rather abstract discussion by stating what the facts are about God's dealing with us and then trying to explain them? Surely we should know whether God guides us if we are talking about anything real? Or if we do not know, is this because he really does not guide us but we dare not admit even to ourselves that the Emperor has nothing on at all?

The Incarnational Deist will be peculiarly sensitive to this difficulty which indeed is "where he came in"; but I believe he need not be too timid at this particular stage in rebutting it firmly. It is indeed perfectly possible and indeed likely that God can guide people without their explicit knowledge of it; and there is nothing philosophically disreputable about this, provided it really is guidance and not evidence of Christianity which is being sought. There need be no epistemological difficulty about supposing that when people pray for guidance God responds by, as it were, feeding ideas

[1] See above, p. 16.

into their minds, letting them draw upon His wisdom, that is, inspiring them to choose better than they would otherwise have done. If they were sincerely praying for guidance their prayer has been answered; and if what they wanted was not guidance as such but a good knock-down argument against the positivist they have no business to be surprised at not getting it. Christ cured people who wanted to be well, not people who wanted a sign.

The moral difficulty about everyday unselfconscious prayer is, this time,[1] much greater than the difficulty about our knowledge. It still seems too artificial to suppose that God rations out the amount of His wisdom He lets people draw upon and that His criteria for deciding how much they "need" are totally different from theirs and unconcerned with the sorts of things in which they are interested. Yet to deny that He guides them at all is a very drastic and negative position for a Christian to arrive at.

Nor has such denial become inevitable: personalism is not exhausted yet. There is still another kind of human guidance to consider. Its caricature looked the most inadequate and least promising of the three as an analogy for prayer for guidance: the case where people do not really want advice at all but someone to back them up;[2] but the worst can be the corruption of the best. Just as to ask for advice need not always be to make oneself a doormat,[3] so to ask for support need not be hypocritical. There are some people whom one does not exactly look on as advisers in the sense that they are more expert, more mature, or more objective than oneself, but whose participation in some sense one would always want in making any important decision. If asked why, one would have to answer, "Because it would hurt their feelings horribly to leave them out" or something of that kind, but this is a negative and inadequate way of expressing something much more positive. It is not a kind of touchiness and if it is a kind of

---

[1] cf. above, p. 72–3.
[2] See above, p. 76.
[3] See above, pp. 78.

jealousy it is like the kind which the Ten Commandments ascribe to God.

Three different examples may illustrate this in different aspects. First, one has some close friends whom one sees constantly. One would be absolutely staggered if one morning the post brought a little printed card informing one that they had changed their address, and only a little less surprised if suddenly they coolly said, "We have decided to move house". Instead of being told about the decision as something outside one's own life one will be allowed and expected to feel a concern over it, almost to be concerned in it. Sometimes one will be able to watch it taking shape. One will wish a friend luck, with whatever mixed feelings, when he goes for an interview for a post the other side of the country. In any case, something definite is being asked of one, something which one could give or withhold. One could find oneself deeply opposed to the decisions one's friend was making, not just humanly regretful for one's own sake but convinced of their unwisdom, and then both project and relationship would be to some degree under pressure. To tell a friend of a new enterprise is not just to inform him but, however inexplicitly, to ask his blessing; which there are many ways of bestowing, not all of which use words. When such blessing is forthcoming the person making the decision is strengthened in his undertaking and has truly given his friend a part in it.

Secondly, two people have a grown-up child, a fully responsible person with his own home and his own life. He is in no way under their authority any more and they do not expect him to be, but he would never do something really drastic such as getting married or changing his career without some reference to them. Filial duty would insist that he informed them, in some special circumstances he might ask for advice, but neither of these is the present point. The suggestion is that part of what it means to say "He gets on well with his parents", that is, has a satisfying personal relationship with them, is that he lets them know what he is up to, tells them about his hopes and fears, does not shut them out of his life. Again it would be misleading to say that they guided him, but still more misleading to deny that they helped him in making decisions.

The third example is a husband and wife who have a difficult problem to solve. Not only do they solve it together, but afterwards they are not even sure who has contributed what to the decision. Certainly each has helped the other, and certainly neither would dream of coming to a decision of this kind without the other's help. This is not only or mainly for reasons of efficiency, but because to act in isolation would be an infringement of trust. They do not look on themselves as self-sufficient beings leading independent lives, but as complementary to one another.

The application of these examples to the problem of human relationship with God is not far to seek. The point of each of them is not the asking of a specific favour but the maintenance of the relationship itself, but it is not a misnomer to speak in terms of help and even of guidance, for the decisions which are made are influenced by the support of the other person and might not be exactly the same, certainly would not feel the same, without it. One person puts himself and his plans in another person's hands. It may be thought that we cannot helpfully compare these human relationships with our relationship to God because they are all voluntary. Though it may be unthinkable that we should withhold our confidence from close friends, parents, husband or wife, it is at least possible; whereas any Christians must realise that he can have no secrets from God. He is in God's hands: he cannot "put" himself there. In practice, however, people are often very far from consciously giving their confidence to God, and it is not unreasonable to say that their actual relationship with Him is as voluntary as their actual relationship with their parents. They can choose to ask His blessing. What is being suggested is that the best way to understand prayer for guidance is as a conscious and willing acceptance of God's presence when one is making decisions. One offers Him one's choices and plans, exposing them to the risk of His disapproval, but in the lively hope that He will bless one, both in their making and their execution. To come to value the blessing more than the plans is to seek to do His will. This is by no means a way of saying that one does not or should not pray for guidance, but it interprets this prayer as a manifestation of a relationship rather than as a more or less technical request. It does not even rule out the legitimacy of the technical request on occasion, but it avoids taking this concept as typical.

I do not think this approach contains anything which need horrify the Incarnational Deist, but the question of course is whether it meets the difficulties. The requirements are that real help should be given, so that it is legitimately called guidance; and yet that personal freedom should neither be impaired, nor safeguarded only by the human limitations of the help. In the kinds of "guidance" which have just been illustrated the element of asking some external person for specific advice is minimised, but it is not minimised by simply reducing the amount of guidance given. It can be described by saying that one person is enabled to draw on another person's resources so as to decide better than would be possible alone; but it is not like having a sort of fund handed over to one, but more like having latent powers of one's own drawn out. Or rather, it is too individualistic to speak of powers "of one's own". The point is that *new* resources have developed, they have not just been pooled. Far from suffering any loss of freedom, one is more of a person than before. Above all, it is not the human limitations of this kind of help that prevent it from pauperising one; on the contrary, its possibilities are endless. They could indeed be infinite, if the other person with whom one was in relationship turned out Himself to be infinite.

CHAPTER SIX

Means of Grace

In the pursuit of the argument about human relationships with God the attempt has been made to avoid saying: logically divine guidance ought to pauperise us, *but* God is not like other people and His guidance unlike theirs makes us more truly ourselves. Now the discussion has reached a point at which it becomes legitimate to say something like this instead: there is a kind of human guidance which does not pauperise but makes us more truly ourselves, *but* of course being human it is limited and incomplete. Two human beings cannot be completely identified with one another's interests, they still to some extent interfere with one another's freedom, they are not completely united any more than they are completely wise. God transcends these human limitations and in relationship with Him one can come to transcend them too. This is paradoxical. It is not only beyond human capacity, it is beyond human understanding: but it is a paradox which extends and expands the argument by which we reached it, not one which simply contradicts human logic. In both the argument which has been avoided and the argument which has been proposed there is a "but" after which one begins to say how different God is from human beings; but in the one case the mystery is dragged in to avoid a difficulty, whereas in the other it is the climax of the argument.

By now it is becoming evident that to say as much as this encroaches upon ground which the Incarnational Deist as such cannot explore; and what has been said will presently need to be taken further, beyond where he can follow.[1] But first there is a notable lop-sidedness

[1] See below, p. 105.

in his picture of the Christian life as presented so far, and this lop-sidedness he can do a great deal to correct, still within the bounds of a characteristically deistic attitude.

The personalism which has been explored on behalf of the Incarnational Deist is vulnerable to the charge that it remains individualistic and even strangely subjective. It looks like a kind of doctrine of assurance: the Incarnation seems to fulfil the role of giving the individual a guarantee that after all God is concerned with the world in spite of appearances. Accept this guarantee and he can enter, blindly but confidently, into "personal relationship" with the Almighty in his daily life: he can hope to begin to "do justly and love mercy and walk humbly" with his God. But is this only for his own comfort? On the one hand, does it make room for disinterested worship and for the "simple loving look at God"[1] which Kirk was wont to emphasise? On the other hand, where do other people come into the picture?

In theory the Incarnational Deist is far from being subjective in his emphasis on response to God as revealed in Christ rather than on some individual pipeline: on allegiance rather than on awareness; on serving God rather than enjoying special feelings. But in practice he will still tend to find worship very difficult. In so far as he really is a kind of deist it will always be hard for him to find objective content in the idea of God as alive and present. Vagueness and lack of actuality will continue to beset his attempts to offer himself simply to God in praise and adoration. If he keeps his head he will see why this is so and up to a point accept it, but he is bound to be unhappily aware of his divergence from one main stream of Christian tradition here, and the conscious lack of what is often called faith may make him either despond or plunge unawares into a religion of works, letting his would-be piety turn into moralism.

This can be rectified, but not by solitary concentration. If the individualism of Incarnational Deism can be corrected, this trouble about objectivity can be much mitigated. It may sound paradoxical to affirm that the more deistic one's Christianity is, the more dependent

[1] *Vision of God*, cf. pp. 409, 437.

one is upon the Church. Surely Deism is a "low-church" heresy, and the Body of Christ a "high-church" speciality? Perhaps it is simply a case of a wheel coming full circle; but certainly some explanation is called for.

The point of Incarnational Deism was precisely to locate some kind of body or "vehicle" for God, so that one could talk validly about His activity, without having to make flimsy assumptions or vague suppositions of His presence wherever one would find His presence convenient. Nothing could meet this need more directly than God the Son Incarnate if one can believe in Him. Christian apologetic endeavours to give reasons for such belief; but there is no Christian apologetic, nor could there be, which simply isolates Christ as God's only vehicle. God did not just visit the world for a given stretch of time and go away again, any more than He created it at a given moment and left it to its own devices. If Incarnational Deism insisted that He did, it would be no more convincing than ordinary Deism, for there is no evidence for such a unique visit except evidence which includes a good deal more. The Gospel was prepared for and followed up: though "followed up" is a thin way of describing the fact that it was *preached*, and is still preached, by a community which claims to be animated by Christ's spirit and to be in some sense his present Body. To call the Church "the extension of the Incarnation" is a specific theory which need not here be explored; but at least one must say this, that unless the Church was and is what I have been calling Christ's "vehicle", then we have no adequate reason to suppose that he ever had a physical "vehicle" at all. To believe in Christ without the Church is to cut off the branch one is sitting on.

Once again Deism is wearing thin, but there is some substance in it still. It is turning out to be an attitude of mind rather than a theory: not a sceptical denial that God acts in the world, but a refusal to assume His presence irresponsibly, a conviction about which way the onus of proof lies. If one is blessed or cursed with this attitude of mind, one will keep on looking for the concrete rather than the abstract, the specific rather than the vague, the objective rather than the subjective, to give solidity to one's religious faith. Perhaps Deism is indeed a "low-church" heresy, for the reason that the Deist who remains fully a Christian will only be able to maintain his position with the support of certain traditionally "high-church" emphases on a visible church, and on plenty of outward public manifestations of divine realities. He is aware of the inadequacy of his own resources; and it will be natural to find himself depending, much more than the believer of pantheistic temperament who readily sees God everywhere, upon the Church as his present tangible point of contact with God's grace.

But to speak of the Church in this way is not nearly precise enough. The meaning of the word "church" can be anything from the architectural to the metaphysical. It can here be taken to mean "the continuing Christian community", in open evasion of the question about which denomination or group of denominations is to be entitled to call itself "the Church", so that the more Wittgensteinian activity of asking not for the meaning but for the use may be pursued.

The Church potentially puts the believer in touch with the Deity in at least four overlapping ways: through human ministry, through public worship, through the Bible, and through the sacraments. The first is of incalculable importance but will be seen by the Deist as indirect. His gratitude will be no less to those Christians who have the gift in their words or simply in their lives of making one aware that they are "on to" something,[1] that Christianity is truly a live option, that Christ is "the food of strong men".[2] Fortified and encouraged, the Christian deist will be more sure that his quest is worthwhile, but he will hope to come to know God better *through* such people, not by directly "abiding in" them.

[1] e.g., "Barth stands in the succession of those, such as Augustine and Anselm, whom Barth himself so seeks to follow, who speak of God in such a way that the spiritual fumblers among us are encouraged to believe that there is indeed a God to speak of." David Jenkins, *Guide to the Debate about God*, p. 73, (Lutterworth Press, 1966). Let it be added that there is much in David Jenkins's own writings which has this effect.

[2] Augustine, *Confessions*, VII: 10.

Public worship is a different matter. "With" is the right preposition here rather than "through" or "in". *With* other people the Christian of deist leanings is not left to his own devices but can join in a process of prayer which is going on anyway however much or little he is able to add to it. He can take his place, identifying himself as far as he is able with the words of the Church even if only at the margin; not stuck in the fear that the gaps in his worship, whether caused by lack of faith or simple lack of concentration, remain inexorably as gaps. The whole Church has an objective offering which is there to be entered into. Such participation is not just a question of feeling more aware of God in a holy place, nor of being carried away by communal emotion, either of which would be wide open to the charge of wishful thinking and take one straight back to the "Emperor's New Clothes" situation. It is rather that awareness ceases to matter so much when it is not all one has, nor indeed what one is primarily aiming at. The objectivity of the offering is what matters. The subjective certainty that God is there to receive it would be agreeable; but the certainty that the offering is being made and that if He is there He will indeed receive it is a sufficient basis to build upon.

This certainty in public worship can be reflected back upon the individual's private prayers. Instead of trying on his own to get in touch with God, he can remind himself that he is still part of the Church and try to align himself with the Church's continuing worship: jumping on to a moving roundabout, so to speak, rather than trying to make a telephone call when the line is bad. So he can hope to evade the pressing dilemma to which he is apt to be peculiarly sensitive, either a mechanical recital of set prayers, or a psychologically unsound attempt to work up subjective awareness. He can treat awareness as a bonus without being afraid of its absence or of its presence; and in offering himself, whether in his own words or other people's, he can know himself part of a common enterprise. He need no longer look on himself as an inadequate launching pad for "the flight of the alone to the Alone".

To many Christians such prayer will still seem pitifully limited. It takes no proper cognisance of the fact that the prayer of the Church is to be "to the Father, through the Son, in the Holy Spirit",[1] for this is a threshold which the Incarnational Deist as such cannot cross. It will have to be attempted later: meantime, there is more to be said about the Church at the present level. The Bible and the Sacraments have yet to be introduced into the picture.

There are Christians still who have been brought up to set the Bible over against the Church. They have been wont to look on it as the way *par excellence* by which the individual can get in touch with God for himself, even sometimes as a kind of stick with which he can beat the Church should it become overbearing. But this cannot work in the long run, because, as has frequently been pointed out, the Bible is the Church's book. They are not two rival or even two alternative vehicles of the knowledge of God, for they have not two separate origins. The Bible was written by Churchmen, what they wrote was selected by Churchmen and handed on from Churchmen to Churchmen through the generations. In so far as it constitutes an appeal from the present-day Church in its lop-sidedness and inspiration it is to an earlier Church also inspired and lop-sided. This is not to be deplored. What is lost in verbal inerrancy is gained in continuity of community.

C. F. Evans puts the position beautifully in his book on the Lord's Prayer, drawing the sting of his negative answer to the question of whether we can know what words the Lord taught. Whether one goes all or only some of the way with his radicalism, one can find his way of linking Bible and Church profoundly illuminating. Using a completely different terminology, he seems to explain with nicety what the concept of a *vehicle* of God's presence could mean, in this context, to an Incarnational Deist.

[1] See below, p. 208. For bringing this point home to me in a different context I am grateful to Dr. Henry Cooper.

Incarnation [he says,][1] would seem to mean more
than that God unites himself with human nature and
human conditions simply in the figure of Jesus for
his lifetime, the union to be dissolved so far as we
are concerned once that life is over. God has also
committed himself to our human nature and human
conditions in what men do with the words and deeds
of Jesus as they receive them for their salvation, and
as they use them as the guide of their lives. What we
have in the gospels is the result of this union – not
the naked words of Jesus, but those words as they
have become through the work they have done in
men. There would seem to be no way back to a confident use of the gospels for our spiritual illumination,
guidance, and nourishment, unless this truth is boldly
grasped. The necessity of grasping it appears from the
fact that even the simplest and most repeated act of
the Christian, the recitation of the Lord's Prayer,
cannot now be just a repetition of what Jesus once
taught, precisely in the words in which he taught it,
but only the recitation of what has resulted from the
interpenetration of the words of Jesus with the minds
and spirits of his first disciples.

Likewise in reading any part of the Bible, New
Testament or Old, the Christian of deist leanings need
not stick in the sceptical assumption that each new
generation is getting further and further away from God's
only real link with the world,[2] nor need he on the other
hand court discouragement by supposing that were he
a proper Christian he would be hearing a direct individual
message from God through His Word. Rather he can
read or listen in the conviction of being still a member of
God's people, entering into the continuity of their
tradition, whenever he happens to be alive and however
faint his own specific religious experience. He can resort
to the scriptures for long-term spiritual nourishment,
not for ancient lore nor instant inspiration, and will

[1] *The Lord's Prayer*, p. 15. (S.P.C.K., 1963).
[2] cf. Ranke's famous assertion that every generation is equidistant from
eternity.

incidentally be much more able to take the rough with the smooth. Nor need he be too mystified by the double use of "Word of God" for the Bible and for the Second Person of the Trinity. In the sense of "means of communication" to the individual through the continuing community neither usage need be either far-fetched or weakly metaphorical.

A suspicion may enter in here that God's presence has after all not been located but merely excused from appearing. If every Christian is putting the onus on the others to find the reality of God's Word, they are once again all back in the Emperor's New Clothes situation. Each individual disclaims all responsibility and lays it upon the rest: a sort of "jam yesterday, jam tomorrow, but never jam today". Fortunately this picture does not entirely correspond with the facts. The people of God has constantly thrown up particular individuals who have not repudiated responsibility but have claimed to hear God's Word for themselves. It has been spoken as "Thus saith the Lord": once as "But I say unto you". So the tradition to be passed on has consisted of particularities, not generalities. This is what gives the individual Christian who lacks such a clear message of his own the right to hope that he is indeed, through the Church, in touch with God's Word, though he has no idea what it would be like to be God's mouthpiece. The testing of such claims is no easy matter, but it depends upon their moral and historical coherence, not upon having a similar experience for oneself. It is a matter of objectively putting one's trust where one best can, not of subjective proddings of one's inner consciousness.

Before moving on to ask where the Sacraments come into all this, it may be a help to pause and attempt to consolidate what has already been said about the Word, by setting alongside each other two exceedingly different writers who happen to form an effective comparison with each other and with the present view. Both emphasise the importance of a faithful and functioning community, but in contrasting ways.

D. Z. Phillips in *The Concept of Prayer* is deeply concerned to achieve a more worthy, a more "supernatural" understanding of God, who he insists is not just another being like ourselves. His conviction that "prayer is not a conversation"[1] will encourage the Incarnational Deist who has found in practice, maybe to his disappointment, that indeed it does not seem to be. Yet prayer is real, and it is in the continuing religious community that it can be learnt and practised.[2] In one's own religious tradition one learns to talk about God, to pray to Him, and even to enter into personal relationship with Him. There is much here which anyone in sympathy with the present approach[3] must find congenial and important.

But with all this, indeed as the foundation of all this, there is a deep-rooted opposition to the anthropomorphism to which the Incarnational Deist wants to cling. Professor Phillips's emphasis on the community comes from quite a different direction, a direction learnt from Wittgenstein. In this emphasis, the community is the place where language is learnt, and no kind of language, religious or any other, has meaning apart from the way in which it is taught and learnt. This leads to the curious corollary: that God Himself, far from being like us "an existent among existents, and an agent among agents"[4] is not really a participant in human community at all, for we cannot share concepts with Him.[5] Professor Phillips insists that "God's ability to enter into relationship with men is not made possible by His being able to participate in a shared language; an ability which cannot be separated from the learning of a language".[6] The reason why prayer is not a conversation, then, is that God, unlike persons, "does not *use* language".[7]

Is not this somewhat defeatist, making God less real than ourselves, not more? Of course it would be foolish to try in a few paragraphs to demolish the argument of a whole book: foolish, and also ungrateful, when much that Professor Phillips says about worshipping a "super-

[1] *The Concept of Prayer*, p. 50, (Routledge & Kegan Paul, 1965.)
[2] ibid., p. 37.
[3] e.g., p. 86ff above.
[4] ibid., p. 83.
[5] ibid., e.g., the treatment of anger on p. 47.
[6] ibid., p. 50.
[7] ibid., p. 73.

natural" God is assuredly a valuable corrective to the limitations in the outlook of the Incarnational Deist. But without attempting to demolish one can compare, and hope by such comparison to bring out more clearly what one has said so far; and one can put in a plea for further clarification and elaboration of a theory one finds stimulating but open to criticism.

Professor Phillips's doctrine of God is certainly somewhat elusive. It seems to stress the analogical character of all talk about God to such an extent as to leave us with no practical idea of Him at all, almost with no right to say "Him" instead of "It". To try to relate ourselves to a Deity who will not be related to us seems not only an impossible exercise, but to have lost all touch with the biblical concept of the Covenant. If the God of our tradition is supposed to have inaugurated that tradition by condescending to enter into community with His people, how can His followers deny such community without destroying their tradition itself? Most people realise that "In the beginning was the Word" is an analogical way of speaking which does not depend on ascribing vocal chords to God; but surely it has something rather more literal than analogical to do with God's means of communication? God's Word as spoken "in divers times and divers manners" and then ultimately by His Son is too basic a Christian concept for anthropomorphism to be so firmly ruled out. If it has to be accepted that "God does not participate *in* any language"[1] there seem to be two layers of analogy in talking about His Word, between which meaning is bound to get lost.

The other fundamental Christian concept which Professor Phillips seems to approach but eventually repudiate is the concept of the Church as the Body. One tends, perhaps naively, to assume that the reason why it is in the Church that one can learn to pray and to know God is that the Church remains, more or less adequately, as what I have been calling God's *vehicle*. He uses it for His purposes on earth. Christian life in the Church accordingly seeks to relate itself to an objective Someone about whom the tradition which being

[1] *The Concept of Prayer*, p. 50f.

handed down is held to be true not false, sound not distorted, in so far as it goes back continuously to reliable origins and is still being fed from the same source. Yet Professor Phillips seems to suggest that the tradition is somehow self-enclosed; in which case how can it ever be criticised or validly reformed? Did Paul know that he worshipped the same God as Abraham by knowing something about God Himself, or just by knowing that he stood in the same tradition?[1] This theory of the identity of a religious tradition reminds one of Locke's theory of the identity of a person, that the "same person" is actually constituted by his continuous memory. Bishop Butler's criticism seems to be relevant to both: "Consciousness of personal identity presupposes, and therefore cannot constitute, personal identity; any more than knowledge, in any other case, can constitute truth, which it presupposes."[2] Likewise consciousness of worshipping the same God presupposes that there is a God to be worshipped about whom people can be more or less right or wrong. If not, participation in a tradition cannot relate man to God. This stipulation must become more urgent rather than less when the concept of the Body is developed into its sacramental meanings.[3]

By contrast Dr. Artur Weiser in his magisterial book on the Psalms,[4] while emphasising that it is in the public worship of the holy community that the individual finds God, simply has no apparent doubt that it is an objective God that he finds. "The phrase 'behold the face of God' is derived from the theophany as the climax of the rites performed in the cult when the worshipper experiences the presence of his God with joy and trembling."[5] To this theme he repeatedly returns; but in his profound concern to show that the Temple worship was personal not mechanical, he does not seem to feel the need to show that it was objective not subjective. He does not give full-scale consideration to the question of how literally he takes the idea of the "theophany", the appearance of

---

[1] *The Concept of Prayer*, p. 25f.
[2] *Dissertation of Personal Identity*, Gladstone ed., p. 388.
[3] See below, p. 102.
[4] *The Psalms*, English translation, S.C.M., 1962.
[5] p. 157, commenting on Psalm 11 : 7.

God. Sometimes he mentions prophetic oracles given on behalf of the Almighty;[1] sometimes the veiling of God's glory in radiant light[2] or impenetrable cloud;[3] sometimes what seems to be an inward experience of the worshipper;[4] but it is not to his purpose to worry about how the worshipper was to know that he was not deluding himself. His concern is to show, in psalm after psalm, how the cult gave the individual believer assurance of God's presence and forgiving grace. The kind of deistically-inclined individual who aspires to believe in God, to have some sort of faith in Him and even to worship Him *without* conspicuous personal assurance is indeed not Dr. Weiser's problem.

Yet for his insight (expressed of course in quite different terminology) into the way in which the community through the cult could be a *vehicle* of God, it is well worth quoting here a passage from his book as a way of both summing up the present line of thought and then moving on forthwith to try to take the sacraments into account.

"To satisfy his hunger with the goodness of the holy temple", [explains Dr. Weiser,[5]] means much more than merely being able to share in the delights of the sacrificial banquet; it means above all that the holy God, unapproachable in his sternness, favours wretched man with the nearness of his presence, that the hour which the psalmist spends in the house of God will become for him the material and spatial *pledge* of being near to God in spirit. The cultic apparatus and setting is here not an end in itself but a means to an end and the way to a communion with God which is inwardly alive; it is a *means* of the divine *grace* whereby God gives himself to man, and with his Person the abundance of his salvation.

Most evidently here Dr. Weiser is taking a look forward

[1] e.g., pp. 438, 571.
[2] e.g., p. 395.
[3] e.g., p. 632.
[4] e.g., p. 626.
[5] pp. 463-4, commenting on Psalm 65. Italics mine.
    7

from the old covenant to the New, from the Temple cult to the Christian sacraments. The manner and phraseology in which he does this could be particularly constructive for the Incarnational Deist, for whom the sacraments may be an activity of the Church to be looked upon with a certain amount of suspicion. On the face of it the Church may seem to have the uncomfortable choice of presenting these, the most characteristic of its proceedings, as either naively magical or only subjective again after all, influencing us as mysterious outward applications or as merely inward impressions. It is understandable if the Christian of deist inclination feels vaguely unhappy here. But if he stops at this point he has overlooked a potentially major strengthening of his position.

He has been looking for a vehicle of God's presence; and what is this, in more traditional words, but a means of grace? The sacraments, like the Incarnation, are something physically given; and their authority is the same as that of the Incarnation itself. They are part of the basic tradition which the Church is handing down. The very fact of becoming a member of the Church is not left indefinite and uncertain, like being "in" or "out" of a clique: it is sealed with a material rite needing real water for its performance, of which people can make sure. Even if someone only *thinks* he believes, he *knows* he belongs to the body of believers if he knows that he was baptised.[1] He may never choose to align himself with them; he may seek, as a Quaker for instance, to align himself with them without baptism; but there is this firm objective foundation for him to take his stand on if he will.

It may be said that this is quite inadequate, that the sacrament of Holy Baptism means much more than this; but it probably does not to the Incarnational Deist, especially if he is a layman. His own baptism is generally something seemingly over and done with which he cannot remember. There is apparently nothing he can do about baptism now except perhaps enter into con-

[1] Mr. Hugh Dickinson brought out very clearly the connection between baptism and belonging in an article in *Theology* (August 1966), pp. 347–8.

troversy about the practice of Christian initiation; for curiously enough, when this is a sacrament which lay people can even if necessary administer, they do not often tend to feel that the positive theory of it is really their concern. It is easy, for those who are not called upon to attend many christenings, to hover somewhat vaguely between the idea that Baptism is a passport to heaven and that it is the asking of God's blessing for a particular baby; for to die and be risen with Christ is a concept which one can only make one's own when one has left any kind of deism far behind. Until then, to have become a member of Christ's Body is at least a valid and positive idea to seize hold of.

The Eucharist impinges upon one in a different way. Every active Christian has got to take some present line about it, even a negative one; and often of course this line will consist in clinging tenaciously to the sacramental teaching one was first given, which one probably received (unlike the usual candidate for Baptism) at an impressionable age. But what one clings to tenaciously one does not always find helpful. If a would-be Christian is disposed to look on the life of the Church with a deistically-inclined detachment or even embarrassment, there are some aspects of ordinary Christian teaching about the Eucharist which can only increase this malaise. Mystification, mumbo-jumbo and even a suspicion of cannibalism can seem to haunt the outward aspects of the sacrament; and on the other hand it is evident how easily the inward aspect could be self-induced.

It is from this impasse that the familiar phrase *means of grace*, if it is allowed to carry its full weight, can help to let one out. The physical rite, the partaking of bread and wine, is not a magical spell nor a kind of psychological pressure, but a material vehicle for the presence of God, His "real presence" indeed. How after all can any personal relationship be effectively carried on without some such material expression?[1] One needs to utter words, aloud or on paper, to smile or frown, move or keep still; but more than that, one practically needs the handshake or the kiss, the formal standing up, comfortable

[1] See above, pp. 26–7, 30–1.

sitting or perhaps reverent kneeling, to express oneself or understand what other people are trying to convey. It might be possible to define a sacrament as "a point of intersection of the personal and the material", and if so human life is sacramental through and through;[1] and frequently material things are used as "elements". Wedding rings and badges of rank, prizes, medals and birthday presents are not just attractive objects wanted for their own sake, nor "merely" symbolic like a souvenir "of sentimental value only"; but when given in the approved context are truly a sort of human "means of grace", properly conferring the reality they symbolise,[2] whether a change of status, goodwill, affection, honour or whatever it may be.

Likewise a relationship with God which dispenses with all such signs is hardly conceivable,[3] which is surely a large part of the reason why some people feel themselves to be without God's presence: they are trying to achieve it while consciously or unconsciously denying it all actual means of expression. The less one is aware of special graces the more one needs to make use of appointed means, not as an alternative method of giving oneself good feelings, but as the way almost literally to "keep in touch".

The Eucharist seen from this point of view is the appointed means, the vehicle par excellence. It may be said to carry on the role that the Incarnation has supremely fulfilled, of "giving God a body": in Professor Dodd's words, an "organic instrument of His Personality".[4] There is no need to say deistically that God has no foothold in the universe, for He has given this *pledge* of

---

[1] The best example, the physical side of marriage, I have suggested elsewhere: *Christian Marriage*, "Christian Knowledge Booklets", (S.P.C.K., 1965); Appendix 4 to *Marriage, Divorce and the Church*, p. 128, (S.P.C.K., 1971); "Marriage and Grace", *Theology* (December 1969), p. 537.

[2] The line of thought in this paragraph owes a good deal to Professor D. D. Evans's application of Austin's theory of performatives in *The Logic of Self-Involvement*, (S.C.M., 1963).

[3] The Quakers are not really an exception here: their proceedings are full of a sober and impressive order akin to ritual. In any case with their emphasis on the Inner Light they are far from the situation of the deist for whom the problem is most acute.

[4] *Moffat New Testament Commentary on Romans*, p. 194, (Hodder and Stoughton, 1932).

His presence. "Pledge" is a useful word here, for it is much less metaphorical than many. To celebrate the Eucharist is among other things to claim a promise, an empirical human promise which we believe to have been made. With whatever reason we believe that the human Jesus Christ was God Incarnate, with the same reason we can believe that the promise was the New Covenant between God and Man: putting our faith, not in the verbal inerrancy of Scripture, but in the total impact of the tradition handed down by the Church.

Therefore if one can be an Incarnational Deist one can at least advance to be a Sacramental Deist. The much-quoted verse ascribed to Queen Elizabeth can be seen as having distinct not equivocal meaning:

> His was the word that spake it,
> He took the bread and brake it,
> And what his word did make it,
> I do believe and take it.

The idea is explained more prosaically by Professor Leenhardt:[1] "Things are what God makes of them: they are what they realise of His active will". To partake of the Eucharist is to avail oneself of a means of grace, made so by God's appointing bread and wine to be vehicles of His presence in the Church.[2]

Nor is there any reason why such an approach should confine one to a partial and lop-sided Eucharistic theory. The complete tradition can assuredly be given full scope, with its interlocked themes of thanksgiving, covenant, supper, communion, real presence: none separable from the key concept of offering or sacrifice, which in recent years has been newly appreciated and explored both by Catholic and Protestant.[3] Only the two extremes of a mere memorial service, and of a quasi-magical transformation of the elements into actual but imperceptible flesh and blood, seem refreshingly irrelevant.

---

[1] Cullman & Leenhardt, *Essays on the Lord's Supper*, p. 47.

[2] e.g., Leenhardt, p. 49.

[3] A process which has culminated in the recent joint statement.

The greatest emphasis will tend to be laid on the corporate aspect of this sacrament: Christ known and available to his people in the breaking of bread. One will want to stress that the Last Supper was not a sudden and isolated piece of ceremony, the institution of a brand-new rite, but the illumination and transformation of the familiar way in which their unity expressed itself and was built up. It is continuous surely both backwards and forwards with the other meals they ate together, with the feeding of the five thousand, the supper at Emmaus and the bread and fish by the lakeside: unique in its significance not its character. But what authenticates the continuing gift of Christ's presence in the bread and wine is his death and resurrection. He could give his body and blood because he did give his body and blood, and he could give them by his chosen material means of a sacramental meal because by rising from the dead he had shown himself Lord of the created universe. Dr. Farrer most illuminatingly expounded[1] the point this paragraph has been feeling after: "He gave them the sacrament by eating with them; he made it their salvation by his death".

For a Christian to join in this sacrament, to "do this", it is not just to obey an isolated command, at the mercy of scholars for its proper interpretation, but to enter into a tradition. The picture of the Breaking of the Bread in the Catacomb of S. Priscilla in Rome is not only a picture of fascinating antiquity, but a picture of one's fellow Christians doing what the Church still does. In this "means of grace" God's presence is authentically localised. One can claim to be able after all to "identify grace" in the sense of finding a physical place where it is focused. The continuing enquiry about what it can mean to say that by grace God is in us and we in Him is of course not confined to this paradigm case, but it is at least inseparably linked with the enquiry about how we can partake of His body and become part of His body.

---

[1] In an essay, "The Eucharist in 1 Corinthians", *Eucharistic Theology* then *and now*, (S.P.C.K. Theological Collection), p. 31. To this essay I am immensely indebted.

THE BREAKDOWN OF DEISM

CHAPTER SEVEN

Deism at a Loss

A deistic Christianity has not shown itself unable to identify grace; but it is not going to be able to confine grace within deistic limits. This need not invalidate what has been said so far. It does not matter that an incarnational, even a sacramental, deism cannot do justice to the whole Christian doctrine, so long as it can do the job for which it was propounded. If a would-be Christian is unable by looking about him to find a diffused God or a diffused grace, if immanence means very little to him, it is proper to let him wear deistic blinkers to direct his gaze in the most useful direction. If what he is looking for, a specific vehicle of God's presence, can be found by narrowing rather than broadening his vision, so well and good. It does not follow that he may one day have to take the blinkers off again.

Even already, within the limits of a deistic outlook, he has had glimpses of other facts about personal relationships, of kinds of unity[1] which from his point of view he could not fully explore.[2] What is going to bring forward the day when such exploration must be undertaken and pursued into theological territory is not abstruse philosophical studies but plain reading of the New Testament. The Incarnational Deist has located his "specific vehicle of God's presence" in the person of Jesus Christ. He will soon find that he cannot do any kind of justice to what the biblical writers themselves say about Christ without being led quickly on a very long way beyond even the most incarnational version of Deism. So far he has been trying to give a use to the language of personality and individuality as applied to God conceived as a living

[1] See above, pp. 83–5.
[2] See above, p. 86.

active Being without a physical body. He has been able
to simplify the issue by concentrating entirely on the
"separate person" aspects of Christianity: not unfairly,
because these aspects are truly present.[1] Now it is high
time to face the fact that the very same sources which
suggest that God can be thought of as having some
foothold in the physical world seem to undercut any
talk of Him as "*a* person" faster than they justify it.
The Incarnation poses at least as many problems about
the relationship of God and man as it solves, for it was
the Incarnation itself that set apparently balanced and
intelligent men talking about Christ abiding in us and
we in him, about dying and being risen with Christ,
about being in the Spirit. As D. M. Baillie pointed out,[2]
the concept of "Not I, but the grace of God" is not only
Christian but distinctively Christian, by contrast on the
one hand with the characteristic absorption of Brahma
and on the other with the independence of Islam.

Nor is this emphasis confined to certain specialised
strands of New Testament thought. Indeed if there is
one philosophical theme which can be said to run right
through the variegated writings, it is this theme of
"personal immanence". From the Pauline and Johannine
writings it hardly needs illustrating. It is present in
I Peter: "He himself bore our sins in his body on the
tree, that we might die to sin and live to righteousness.
By his wounds you have been healed."[3] It is to be found
in a haunting passage in the Epistle to the Hebrews:
"For the word of God is living and active, sharper than
any two-edged sword, piercing to the division of soul
and spirit, of joints and marrow, and discerning the
thoughts and intentions of the heart. And before him no
creature is hidden, but all are open and laid bare to the
eyes of him with whom we have to do."[4] None of these
writers seems to have envisaged God as an individual
distinct person straightforwardly over against the individual Christian; nor, which is very much to the point,

[1] See above, p. 19.
[2] *God was in Christ*, p. 123, (Faber, second edition, 1955).
[3] 2: 24.
[4] 4: 12-13. I am grateful to Canon R. P. Dodd for particularly directing
my attention to the relevance of this passage. See below, p. 191.

do the Synoptics, for all their emphasis upon the heavenly
Father caring as a human father does for his beloved
children. Whatever Christ meant by referring to himself
as the Son of Man; whatever he was claiming in forgiving
sins not committed, humanly speaking, against himself;
whatever we may believe he announced about the
atoning effects of his own death: there is material here
which a severely individualistic view of personality will
find it hard to assimilate, all of which bears out the
conviction that "personal immanence" is a New Testament
theme in a fundamental way.

The most telling Synoptic example is the deceptively
simple "Inasmuch" saying.[1] "As you did it to one of the
least of these my brethren, you did it to me", with its
frightening converse: where a triple identification seems
to be asserted between the King who is judge, Christ
himself, and the unfortunates on earth who have been
his representatives, it seems, in no mildly metaphorical
sense. Much of Christian ethics is an attempt to take
this "parable" seriously; to reckon with the likelihood
that in God's eyes the way we treat each other is in
truth the way we treat Christ. It was the same piece of
live theology which converted Paul, when he heard the
risen Lord identify himself with his persecuted people.[2]
But such identification, though we are used to it now,
carries implications which go beyond ethics into metaphysics. The reasons Christians have for their belief
are not reasons for believing in a deistic God who is
straightforwardly a distinct person.[3] If He is related to
people at all, it is not just by confronting them face
to face.

Ethically such understanding is extremely attractive.
Not only does it enliven in practice our appreciation of
one another's value: it helps us to go a stage further in
dealing with the insistent question of the nature of
God's moral claim upon us. Is the demand for perfection
compulsory or optional? How can love be demanded?

---

[1] Matthew 25: 40, 45.
[2] Acts 9: 5.
[3] The typographical device of a capital letter H for pronouns referring
to the Deity is a useful reminder that divine personality is mysterious.

A personalistic Incarnational Deism can go a long way to answer this[1] by transcending the optional/compulsory dichotomy and speaking in terms of response rather than of obligation. But as long as God is thought of as simply *another* person, however infinitely important, the problem eventually recurs, for maybe one can think twice before entering into this sort of relationship with Him at all? At the human level a husband or wife will look on "duty" as an inadequate way of characterising the claims of married life, and yet there was a stage when to enter into this duty-transcending relationship was a matter of choice. If relationship to God is not likewise to remain in the last resort "optional", some kind of notion of divine "immanence", of God's fundamental and inescapable relatedness to people, is integral to an adequate picture of Christian ethics.[2] The way of thinking represented by the "inasmuch" text makes God's claim part of everyone's life, whether recognised as such or not, rather than an extra perhaps even competitive commitment to be taken on by the pious few.[3] To acknowledge the ubiquity of the claim need be in no way to go back upon previous personalistic insights, but it does further impugn the adequacy of any kind of deism, and demand that the nature of persons should be more thoroughly considered.

The sacramental character of Christianity continues this ambivalence between plurality and unity, the individual and the corporate, which its incarnational character inaugurates. Like the Incarnation, the sacraments provided data for talking about God's grace, they focus it, they fit it as it were into a specific and individual context. As promised means of grace they are something which can be seen with our eyes, and which our hands can handle; they give the Christian claim to encounter God a time and place; they give God a Body. But at the same time, by virtue of all this and not just as a peripheral complication, they set Christians talking about

---

[1] See above, p. 69ff.

[2] I have touched on this in *Law and Love*, p. 82; and in "Moral Choice and Divine Authority" printed in *Christian Ethics and Contemporary Philosophy*, ed. I. T. Ramsey, e.g., pp. 231–2, (S.C.M., 1966).

[3] cf. J. Baillie, *And the Life Everlasting*, p. 276, (Oxford, 1934).

that Body in ways which are very far from being plain
and literal.

In this connection, one of the most vivid statements
of eucharistic doctrine one could find is a pictorial one:
Raphael's so-called *Disputation of the Mass* in the Vatican.
Take it merely as a portrayal of the Roman doctrine of
transubstantiation and one must admire it as a great
picture. Take it less narrowly as a portrayal of the
operation of grace and it reveals the theological intricacies
of the Christian concept with nicety. It shows the heavenly
community in a semi-circle above with the Risen Lord
in the centre, linked with the lower semi-circle of the
community on earth by the Holy Spirit in the form of a
dove. The Spirit seems to pour Himself down upon the
Host in the centre of the picture, establishing as it were
the identity of the Body of Christ in heaven and the
Body of Christ on earth. The two physical manifestations
of Christ's presence, his risen body and his sacramental
body, painted in the same pale colour, are set one above
the other, balancing each other; each as it were the focus
of its own part of the picture, and united by the symbol
of the Spirit. No composition so complex could be more
lucid; but nothing so dependent upon the basically
straightforward concept of a human body could be less
straightforwardly anthropomorphic.

Thought along these lines makes Incarnational Deism
appear not only one-sided but naive, looking blankly at
whole ranges of Christian theology which it cannot
possibly enter. So much the better, it might be said:
rejoice in naivety, curb the fancies of the theologian, shed
the philosopher's predilection for the difficult, start where
the simple believer starts, and enter heaven along with
him. The trouble is that the naivety of Incarnational
Deism is of a somewhat specialised kind, not necessarily
by any means the naivety of the simple believer. If the
simple believer is naive it is in supposing that whole
complexes of unexamined ideas are credible and compatible with one another: providence, grace, the Spirit of
God, and all the while on the other hand the individuality
of man. The Incarnational Deist looks at all this with a
kind of single-minded conviction that things ought to be

clear, and if he is not careful he will shut his mind to real subtleties. His position is of course an artificial one, maybe one which no actual Christian has ever precisely held. The reason for accompanying him so far has been that he has something definite to say: partly negative, a standing warning not to explain difficulties by bringing in fresh difficulties; but partly positive, a limited but distinct personalism. He could be a sort of Virgil to the would-be theologian's Dante: honourable and useful, though only up to a certain stage: to be left behind, not repudiated.

In his company one has been able to abandon any impersonal picture of grace as a thing which God hands over or pours down upon us, and look on it rather as an attitude which He takes up towards us. But now this is not enough. To do justice to the full Christian understanding, grace must somehow be God's activity in us; which brings the whole argument back to where it began, with the unexplained but essential concept of personal immanence to be reckoned with. What the Incarnational Deist's intervention has done, it is to be hoped, is give some justification for a *personalist* theology in spite of the fact that God has no body like other persons and cannot obviously be located in the world around us. But the more one ventilates the notion of "personal" as applied to God, the less one is able to leave "immanence" out of account.

The Christian doctrine which the Incarnational Deist cannot cope with at all is the doctrine of the Holy Spirit. Analogies, more or less moralistic, come to mind. Such a believer is like a motorist, driving steadily along with no comprehension of what goes on under the bonnet, and perhaps never breaking down at all; or, alternatively, he is a reader using a lamp to see by rather than dazzling himself by gazing at the lamp itself. Here it is more to the point to leave out the analogies and the various practical lessons which may be drawn out of them and say that in so far as the Incarnational Deist is scholar as well as believer, he is a scholar working on only part of the available data. Everything that gives a Christian grounds for believing in God, gives him grounds for believing in a God who is more than a Deist can envisage. Part of what Christians have always meant by a personal relationship is that God is somehow present on both sides of the relationship, that He is the God within us as well as the God to whom we pray. "When we cry, 'Abba, Father' it is the Spirit himself bearing witness with our spirit that we are children of God."[1] "And because you are sons, God has sent the Spirit of his son into our hearts, crying 'Abba! Father!'."[2] The difficulty is to get some grasp of what this concept can mean.

When the problem is set out in these terms it can be appreciated that these theologians who have recently been wont to insist that God is not to be thought of as "*a* person" are not necessarily attacking personalism, and frequently conceive themselves even to be speaking in its name. Nor need they be saying anything new-fangled and unorthodox, in spite of the uproar occasioned by *Honest to God*. In spreading the Gospel according to Tillich, Dr. Robinson has most evidently seen himself as picking out neglected aspects of genuine Christianity, not as branching out on his own. Tillich himself in his sermons seems unmistakably a Christian preacher. The current onslaught upon anthropomorphic conceptions of Christianity can be seen as a wholly reputable campaign (incautious and exaggerated at times as campaigns have a way of being) in the interests of a renewed under-standing of the Christian doctrine of immanence.

Several distinguishable points are made which need to be disentangled. First, there has been a fervent insistence that God cannot be just one object among many, or He would not be God. "God is not an object among objects. He transcends the world of objects as well as every subject."[3] "If God were *a* person, he would be one being alongside other beings, and not He in whom every being has his existence and his life."[4]

Secondly, these thinkers have pointed to the character-

[1] Romans 8: 15–16.
[2] Galatians 4: 6.
[3] Tillich, "The God above God", Third Programme talk published in *The Listener* (3rd August, 1961), on which I have drawn because it sets out the case with such lucidity.
[4] ibid.

istic religious statements about God being within us as
well as "over against" us. God is "nearer to each of us
than we are to ourselves. A person is separated from
any other person; nobody can penetrate into the innermost centre of another. Therefore we should never say
that God is a person. And neither the Bible nor classical
theology ever did."[1]

Thirdly, then, one is reminded (with conscious orthodoxy) that the doctrine of the Trinity ought to preclude
any Christian from talking glibly about God as one person
when in any case He is three. "In classical theology the
Latin term *persona* applied only to the three faces of
God as Father, Son, and Spirit."[2]

The argument against calling God "a person" is not
left without a warm affirmation of a personal faith:
"If, however, we say that God as the creative source of
everything personal in the universe is personal himself,
we are right. He cannot be less than his creation. But
then we must make another assertion and say: he who is
personal is also more than personal; and conversely:
he who is more than personal is also personal, namely,
personal for us who are persons."[3] In *Honest to God* and
still more in *Exploration into God* Dr. Robinson likewise
seeks to allay the anxieties of his readers; though it
must be admitted that not all of them have felt reassured.
Immanence is not as obviously compatible with real
personality as individual distinctness is: there is apt to
remain a feeling that the living God has been done away
with. What these writers have shown is that the problem
needs to be faced: for which we must first take a closer
look at the arguments.

The last of them, the Trinitarian one, is not such a
debating point as might be thought. It is not as if someone said, "I told you there wasn't *a desk* in my room:
there are two." It is rather that since Christians do not
with their belief in the Trinity renounce their claim to
be monotheists, they are already trying to affirm some-

[1] ibid.
[2] ibid., cf. *Honest to God*, pp. 39–40, (S.C.M., 1963), and Mark Gibbard,
Why Pray? p. 49, (S.C.M., Centre Books, 1970).
[3] Tillich, "The God above God".

thing peculiar about what divine personality can mean, before anything has been said about relationships between man and God. Or rather, since in historical order it was from relationships between man and God through Christ that the doctrine of the Trinity arose, one may say that the experienced odd characteristics of these relationships are believed to reflect a fundamental oddness in the personal being of God Himself. Immanence of some kind seems to crop up at every stage and every level.[1]

The seemingly more inescapable argument that God must not be made into an object is, to the present writer, much less convincing. May it not be the case that the self-limitation of creation consists in just this, that God condescends to become in a way "one being alongside other beings", for He so to speak puts them there alongside Himself? When at last Christ takes his seat at God's right hand, it is as perfect man, the first fruits of creation, that he takes this place, not simply as the Second Person of the Trinity: and though the "place" is a metaphor, the distinctness and "alongsideness' which it indicates is not.

The crux of the matter is the second argument, that to say that God is not "a person" distinct from ourselves, but part of our very being, is not just a concession to dangerous modern thought but part of what people mean by affirming faith in God at all. The idea of *a* man set over against *a* God like two human beings confronting one another has never been found adequate for long.

More particularly, its inadequacy was insistently set before the Church over half a century ago by a profoundly Christian thinker whose great strength was his balanced appreciation of the concepts both of immanence and of transcendence, and his understanding that a "personal religion" requires both: C. C. J. Webb, later Oriel Professor of the Christian Religion. To his influence indeed Dr. Robinson makes warm acknowledgment;[2] but had his writings been more thoroughly attended to, much of the upheaval over *Honest to God* might have been avoided.

[1] See below, p. 201ff.
[2] *Exploration into God*, p. 20. Also, *Honest to God*, p. 39, n. 5.

8

C. C. J. Webb was certainly a "personalist", but he
patiently endeavoured to show[1] that the expression "the
Personality of God" goes back no farther than the
eighteenth century, and that the traditional Christian
understanding is the Trinitarian conception of "personality *in* God". He summarised his position characteristically
in the "Syllabus", or chapter-analysis, of *God and
Personality* :[2]

> An examination of various accounts of the divine
> nature, undertaken with the view of satisfying ourselves
> whether they could be described as accounts of a
> "personal God", leads to the result that only so far
> as *personal relations* are allowed to exist between the
> worshipper and his God can that God be properly
> described as "personal"; and that such personal
> relations are excluded alike by extreme stress on the
> "immanence" and by extreme stress on the "transcen-
> dence" of the object of worship.

The fashionable heresy of his youth was the sort of
high-minded Idealism which makes little of the individual
and underestimates the importance of reciprocity[3] in
the relationship of God and man; in which it is thought
naive to suggest that the Absolute could love us. Of this
he saw, and stated, the inadequacy.[4] It was the more
remarkable that he did not go headlong to the other
extreme, and that his abidingly significant contribution
to the philosophy of religion should be a profound
analysis, not itself particularly "Idealist", of what goes
wrong when the Christian doctrine of immanence is
neglected. His appeal was not to any particular philosophy
but to the requirements of religious experience itself.
To give the flavour of his thought it is necessary to quote
substantial passages. He bluntly doubted whether religious
people really do

---

[1] *God and Personality*, ch. III.
[2] The first course of his Gifford lectures, 1918.
[3] See above, p. 22.
[4] e.g., *Group Theories in Religion and the Individual*, p. 175ff., (Allen &
Unwin, 1916).

think of God as just another person standing side by
side with them . . . I venture to affirm, [he said,[1]] that
most of us, if we were to guess that any other man or
angel saw and knew, without our consent or privity,
the innermost thoughts of our hearts, should feel that
nothing could be more horrible than such an invasion
as this of the sanctuary of our personality. . . . Yet
such knowledge of "the thoughts and intents of the
heart" all believers in God, at least when religion has
reached a certain level . . . would attribute without
hesitation to him; but I venture to say that, however
much they may tremble at the thought that there is
nothing in them but "is naked and open to him"
"in whose sight the very heavens are not clean", yet
not for one moment do they feel the sense of insecurity
and outrage which they would feel if they believed
their hearts to be exposed to unauthorised prying by a
fellow-creature.

He brings out the point particularly clearly with
reference to the ancient gods of Greece.

Now I think we may say that to take for God a particular person . . . is really inconsistent with the satisfaction
of the need which finds expression for the demand
among ourselves for a "personal God", so far as this
is a really religious demand at all. The Homeric gods,
for example are in one sense inhuman, just because
they are in another sense so human. . . . Between
them and us exists that mutual exclusiveness, which,
as we sometimes complain, sets one finite person for
ever apart from another.[2]

This is all the more interesting in that the same point
has been made more recently in a different context by
Professor W. K. Guthrie[3] in his book *The Greeks and
their Gods*. The distinction between gods and men is
simply a class-distinction, "like that which separated

---

[1] *Problems in the Relations of God and Man*, pp. 147–8. Also *God and Personality*, p. 144; *Religion and Theism*, p. 141, (Allen & Unwin, 1936).
[2] *Problems in the Relation of God and Man*, p. 219.
[3] Laurence Professor of Ancient Philosophy, Cambridge.

the human king or chieftain from the common people".[1]
"That gods and goddesses were thought of in this way,
as Agamemnon or Achilles, Helen or Arete raised
to an even higher degree, brings them in one way closer
to mankind, but in another way emphasises the difference
between them."[2] And from this, with reference to the
Athens of the fifth and fourth centuries B.C., precisely
C. C. J. Webb's conclusion is drawn:[3] "When we speak
of a growing disbelief in the gods, the gods that we mean
are the Olympian dynasty of Homer. These were beings
unsuited by their very nature either to call forth or to
satisfy the deepest religious feelings of men."

It would seem that what human religious need cries
out for is a God whom "we could conceive, even though
it were in a way which some would call 'pantheistic', as
animating the world and entering into our inner life".[4]
It is C. C. J. Webb's belief that the Christian doctrine of
the Trinity meets this need,[5] and he claims that the
doctrine is by no means "merely figurative" but is
"language used, not for the sake of talking, but to express
a real experience".[6] "In the Christian doctrine the life
of the Church is the life of the Spirit, and the Spirit is
the Spirit of the Son, whereby he is the Son; and this
relation of Sonship which has this Spirit for its principle
is regarded as integral to the divine essence."[7] He has
the right to insist that in trying to explain such phrases
as "God in us and we in him" the Christian cannot be
expected to leave out of account "the definitely religious
experience".[8]

There is nothing here which is unfair or unreasonable
and much which is constructive; but those who are
inclined to call themselves Christians, but still practically
and intellectually tentative about the "experience",
will need to move a good deal more slowly. What has

[1] *The Greeks and their Gods*, p. 39 (Methuen University Paperbacks, 1968).
[2] ibid., p. 118.
[3] ibid., p. 255.
[4] *Problems in the Relation of God and Man*, p. 222.
[5] ibid., p. 235. See below, p. 201.
[6] ibid., p. 251.
[7] ibid., p. 249. See below, pp. 206–7.
[8] ibid., p. 251.

been shown is that in Christianity properly understood there is a "pantheistic" strain at least as authentic as the "deist" strain which has been emphasised so far. In a way one has come back to the beginning, though potentially with more understanding; with the Emperor once again, though more humbly, donning his new clothes. Unfortunately there is still a "small child" to query the whole basis of the proceedings. This time it is the philosopher McTaggart who fulfils this role: "But it can't be nice to believe in God, I should think. It would be horrible to think that there was anyone who was closer to one than one's friends."[1] Of course the objection shows a lack of subtlety, a failure to appreciate lofty matters. Of course it is ungracious: it cuts sharply into self-congratulation. But fairly or not, it has its effect. It makes one ask oneself how "nice" it is after all to believe in God, and beyond that it stirs up the old doubt about how *possible* it is to believe in God, understood in this way in sharp contrast to other people alongside us. The affirmation that God is not "a person" distinct from ourselves is thrown back on the defensive; and the persistent assumption that the way to talk theological sense is to point out how different God is from men seems to lose its plausibility with a jerk.

The right response is not to go backwards in a panic, but on. The intervention in its turn assumes a good deal. How close to one after all are one's friends? What is this contrast which is being drawn or denied, in either case hastily, between knowledge of God and knowledge of others? It could be that one reason why orthodox Christians have always tended to be alarmed or uncomprehending at any talk of pantheism has been that they have often had a wholly inadequate understanding of human relationships on which to base any such discussion. It may be suggested that the attempt to combine an adequate account of God's immanence with a still thoroughly "deistic" approach to human persons is apt to lead to an impersonalistic pantheism which is rightly stigmatised as heretical.

[1] G. Lowes Dickinson, *J. M. E. McTaggart*, p. 87, quoted by J. Baillie, *And the Life Everlasting*, p. 274.

CHAPTER EIGHT

Oneself and Others

What is needed here is a little excursion into the recent history of philosophy. The "personalist" in theology cannot get far without a philosophical look at the notions of "person" and "personal relationship", which will take him among some of the ramifications of the traditional "other minds" problem. It must be of moment to him to know, in forming his concept of a person, what have been thought to be the possibilities and difficulties of the knowledge people have of one another; but it has to be admitted that the stages of the development of this problem, until quite lately, have been unconsoling though potentially instructive to the theologian. His particular concern is with the belief that persons can enter into relationship with one another while not losing their identities; and in following the fluctuations of the philosophers' argument about how they can enter into relationship at all he will not necessarily find his theology, his philosophy and his common sense ranged upon the same side.

He does not have to leave his common sense so far behind as to take seriously that radical solipsism which doubts whether belief in the existence of other people is even meaningful. Though the aftermath of logical positivism has left a permanent doubt whether statements which cannot possibly be verified can be said to mean anything, there is no necessity for "other minds" to be jeopardised in this fashion. They need not be regarded as perniciously "metaphysical" entities whose existence can never be verified, for since anybody may be "I" and "I" may be anybody, there is no permanent class of "statements about *other* minds".[1] To put it technically,

[1] See Hampshire, "The Analogy of Feeling", *Mind* (1952). Ayer, *The*

it is a contingent fact who I am, and therefore it at least makes sense for me to suppose that I am *one* of many people each of whom is "I" to himself. But to repudiate the radical doubt about other minds only clears the ground. It shows that one can talk about them, not that one can know them. It does not show what is involved in calling people "other" and yet believing that they are able to get in touch with one another; but if there is confusion here it is bound to confuse all the issues about relationship between man and God.

At the outset the distinctness of human persons sticks out, at least superficially, as an evident fact. Whether or not it is right to emphasise, with the deists, *God*'s separateness from the world, one is obliged to give some recognition to the separateness of people from one another. If one is anything of an individualist it is natural, at any rate since Descartes, to accept this separateness contentedly and begin by regarding persons as more or less encapsulated entities, oysters to be opened. One is in good company in starting here, with the traditional assumption that each person knows his own mind directly and the minds of others indirectly, by analogy. "It is plain", said Berkeley,[1] "that we cannot know the existence of other spirits, otherwise than by their operations, or the ideas by them excited in us. I perceive certain motions, changes and combinations of ideas, that inform me that there are certain particular agents like myself, which accompany them and concur in their production." Likewise Hume: "No passion of another discovers itself immediately to the mind. We are only sensible of its causes or effects. From *these* we infer the passion."[2] Already, with this entirely responsible and apparently unexceptionable way of setting the matter out, a barrier has been set up between one person and another. A good

Foundations of Empirical Knowledge, pp. 162–70, (Macmillan, 1947). It is only fair to add that Professor Ayer has since indicated doubts about this solution, e.g., Preface to second edition of *Language, Truth and Logic*, (Gollancz, second edition, 1946).

[1] Berkeley, *Principles of Human Knowledge*, section 145. See also sections 89, 148.

[2] Hume, *Treatise of Human Nature*, ed. A. Selby-Bigge, Part III, section 1, p. 576.

deal turns upon its removal or penetrability if a satisfactory resolution of the theological tension between evident otherness and needful oneness is to be achieved.

On the assumption that the barrier is crossed by analogy, how does the analogy work? The philosophical equivalent of the "average man" is supposed to suggest at this point that whereas in one's own case one is aware both of a body and of a mind activating it, so in other cases one becomes aware of bodies similar to one's own and infers that they likewise are animated by minds. It is easy enough to show up this argument as very shaky indeed. How can such an impudent generalisation from a single instance hope to be valid? Even if it happens to be a lucky guess it can never be checked, so one has no right to put any weight upon it. In any case we do not put any weight upon it: our knowledge of one another is not like this. Children know, really know, that there are other people, before they look very obviously like them, certainly before they are aware of any such likeness. Is our knowledge of other people first to be dependent upon belief in mirrors, and then to remain for ever unsubstantiated? This was how the problem did indeed present itself to eminent philosophers of a generation ago.

A classic discussion of it was by Professor Price in two articles,[1] in which he argued that physical events occur in such a way as to make one realise that there are other *purposes* in the world besides one's own and so that there are other people; and that in particular, we come across meaningful symbols which are not our own, and so are able to get into *communication* with one another. If this analogical approach is right, this is surely the kind of way in which to handle it in detail. So long as one is convinced that our knowledge of one another is and must be indirect, this account of how the barriers can be climbed over is one for which one can only be grateful; but already when these articles were written it was increasingly coming to stick in people's throats to call our knowledge of others "indirect" at all.

[1] Price, "Our Knowledge of Other Minds", *Proceedings of the Aristotelian Society* (1932). "Our Evidence for the Existence of Other Minds", *Philosophy* (1938).

At this stage in the argument it is necessary for a Christian to "declare his interest", or at least to become aware of it himself. He is committed to the belief that however he may be separated from his fellow men, no barrier blocks him off from God. Whether or not he is "one with God" he is at least "open to" God: this is another datum which for Christian thought has to be set alongside the datum of human distinctness. It is hard to overestimate how deeply one's imagination is coloured, when one has been brought up as a Christian, by the picture of God overlooking all one's thoughts and actions. That one is never really alone is not so much an article of faith subscribed to, as built into the structure of one's thinking. As long as one can believe in God at all, He is practically defined as "Your Father who seeth in secret", as "Almighty God unto whom all hearts be open".

The difficulties in the concept lie fairly quiet because one habitually envisages this direct knowledge as one-way only, God knowing us. They may come to life when one tries to add on the Pauline assurance that one day I shall know even as also I am known. They tend to form part of the general malaise which afflicts Christians if they try to think with any definiteness about Heaven, constituting one more reason why the thought of the next world is apt to be pushed untidily and uncomfortably into some hidden corner of the mind. When a Christian finds John Locke wondering trustfully or Charles Lamb wistfully about how spirits in Heaven communicate with each other by some "perfecter way"[1] or by some "awkward process of intuition"[2] rather than by speech or writing, he is liable to feel a disinclination to look into the matter with any thoroughness. He will be made unhappy, even aghast, by a blunt statement like the following: "Spirits are able to discern spirits by a kind of direct non-sensory perception. The angels themselves, as pure bodiless spirits, presumably have this power in the highest degree."[3] It may seem easier to swallow this

[1] Locke, *Essay Concerning Human Understanding*, Book II, Part XXIII, Paragraph 36.

[2] Lamb, "New Year's Eve", *Essays of Elia*.

[3] H. A. Hodges, *The Angels of Light and the Powers of Darkness*, ed. E. L. Mascall, p. 14, (Faith Press, 1954).

assumption like a pill than to query its acceptability, for it is an unpalatable thought that instead of going steadily on in a way we know works, we ought to be looking out for something different and better which may after all turn out to be a chimera.

In this situation of half-suppressed disquiet it could come as a relief to the theologically-minded to find the problems about the possibility of "direct" knowledge of one another being brought into the open and looked into at a human level by philosophers. At one stage the enquiry seemed to hold out a good deal of promise for Christians. It became a favourite topic of certain highly respected religious thinkers[1] who were characteristically interested in the problem of how we know God, unhappy about the prevalent "indirect theory" of our knowledge of other minds, but basically convinced that we do indeed have knowledge both of one another and of God. For these thinkers Cook Wilson's famous remark, "We don't want merely inferred friends"[2] became a kind of slogan, and it seemed a happy answer to say that since such an inference is both dubious and somehow ignoble, we *must* find, if we look without prejudice, that it is by some kind of direct intuition that we know we are in touch with each other and our Creator. Such intuition, or "rapport", to use C. C. J. Webb's word, not perfect nor infallible but real and reliable, is an attractive postulate for anyone in general sympathy with this Christian point of view. "There is something intrinsically coercive and self-evident", said Professor Farmer,[3] "in the apprehension that I am in that quite distinctive sort of relationship to that quite distinctive sort of entity which I call personal. The whole thing is *sui generis*." Seen in this light, "intuition" is hard to deny without an ungracious

[1] e.g., J. Cook Wilson, "Rational Grounds of Belief in God", printed in *Statement and Inference*, Vol. II, (Oxford, 1926).

C. C. J. Webb, *Our Knowledge of One Another*, (British Academy, 1930).

N. Kemp Smith, "Is Divine Existence Credible?' (British Academy, 1931), printed in *Religion and Understanding*, ed. D. Z. Phillips, (Blackwell, 1967).

H. H. Farmer, *The World and God*, (Nisbet, 1936).

J. Baillie, *Our Knowledge of God*, (Oxford, 1939).

[2] *Statement and Inference*, Vol. II, p. 853.

[3] *The World and God*, p. 14.

repudiation of our experienced relationships with one another; it does what is asked of it in assimilating knowledge of other people and knowledge of God closely but not too closely; and it leaves room for as much qualification and adjustment, as much emphasis that the intuition comes through the physical world, as the facts may seem to require.

Yet, like the 1928 Prayer Book, this "direct theory" of our knowledge of one another, with all its promised theological convenience, has been set aside by those who are not churchmen, and after the passage of time churchmen do not seem disposed to repine. It may be a form of snobbery to refuse to take very seriously what has evidently dated, but it is also a form of good sense to bear in mind that ideas do not generally become dated when they present themselves as real answers to real problems. The "direct theory" was far from being merely jejune. It is not for instance refuted out of hand by the fact that people can be taken in by waxworks. It cannot be said though that the basic concept of "intuition" ever emerged fully and decisively enough as a major and indubitable aspect of our experience to carry the necessary weight in the enterprise of demolishing the apparent barriers between persons. One would still want to ask how we know we have it, how we could *distinguish* "inferred friends" from "directly known" friends, whether we are talking about something like telepathy or only like fluent reading. Otherwise "intuition" seems to be only the name of a problem rather than the answer to it.

It is partly a matter of where the onus of proof lies. By speaking warmly of the *rapport* which certainly can exist in human relationships at their best, I can seem to put the onus upon those who would *deny* to such "rapport" the name of "direct knowledge"; but I have only proposed a usage, not established a theory. The way to establish it would be to set it to work, to show that this concept of "direct knowledge", as distinct from "indirect", gives a specific and satisfying account of human relationships as we find them. One could then hope to go on to make the application to the knowledge of God. But in the absence of such specification one begins to realise that what the "direct theory" did was to put agreeably what the "indirect theory" put uncomfortably: that we find ourselves as separate units; that we somehow manage to discover other beings and enter into relationship with them, never doubting that they are substantially like ourselves; but that this indubitable "knowledge of others" is not very easy to characterise accurately. One is the more tempted to label it "direct", in spite of its more than occasional deficiencies, if one is convinced as a Christian that unmediated knowledge of other persons is something ultimately possible and needful to attain; but it could be that such hopeful labelling of our present knowledge is a temptation to be resisted.

Whether it is to be called "direct" or "indirect", it is still being thought of as an insight to be achieved, as a sort of bridge from one distinct being with his own private inner life to another. The next stage in the argument is to query the entire approach according to which "minds" are cut off from each other in this way. The suggestion is that it is philosophy, not life, which has put up the supposed barriers between people, and that with care philosophy can take them down again. For the theologian this enterprise is full of promise and peril: promise that he is not after all cut off from his fellows and from God, as for a while he was being made to fear: peril that the price he will have to pay is such a reduced understanding of what persons really are that Christian doctrines can get no purchase on them.

The whole "problem of other minds" has gradually come to be seen as a kind of "mental cramp" which can, it is hoped, be "loosened" by a suitable therapy.[1] The prevailing feeling has been of release from threatened deadlock. Just as some older cars with automatic gears used to have a way of seemingly settling into themselves when parked on a downward slope so as to become immovable except when driven backwards, so philosophers had seemed to be getting increasingly stuck in the various ramifications of their direct and indirect theories.

[1] Wittgenstein, *The Blue and Brown Books*, p. 59, (Blackwell, 1958), cf. Hare, Review of Wisdom's *Philosophy and Psychoanalysis*, (Blackwell, 1953) in *Philosophy*, 1954, p. 285.

They were set free, into fresh problems, by the movement begun by the colossal impact of Wittgenstein, delayed by the war, but gathering increasing momentum after it. The general effect has been to shift the attention of philosophers concerned with this topic, not only of those specifically beholden to Wittgenstein, away from "all those inferences, constructions, divinations, those exercises of empathy and sympathy"[1] towards more relaxed enquiry into ways of talking about knowledge of persons considered as a *fait accompli*. With this message that one is not to worry the personalist theologian certainly has no right to assume that he must have a quarrel.

The keyword is "therapy", and the most patient attempt to effect a cure took the form of a long and indeed unfinished series of articles in *Mind* by Professor John Wisdom.[2] His method, putting to use what he had learnt from Wittgenstein, was to analyse in elaborate and discursive detail, mostly in the form of a dialogue between several speakers, how one has come to think oneself in philosophical trouble about knowledge of other minds. The process, it is suggested, has been quite simple. One knows what is going on in one's own mind by introspection. One therefore comes to think what a pity it is that there should apparently be no such faculty for knowledge of others.[3] Some philosophers have even coined the word "extraspection".[4] Without such a faculty, we seem to be cut off from each other: "And when this web is woven, it's hard to be free of it, though it's we who wove it".[5]

The therapy consists in the suggestion that one is making a fuss about nothing. In asking for "extraspection" one is not asking for a faculty that it makes any sense to talk about having. With great care Professor Wisdom describes[6] a phenomenon, a kind of extended telepathy,

---

[1] J. N. Findlay, *Values and Intentions*, p. 73, (Allen & Unwin, 1961).
[2] *Mind*, Vols. XLIX–LII. Eight articles reprinted in "Other Minds", *Proceedings of the Aristotelian Society*, (Blackwell, 1952).
[3] ibid., p. 101.
[4] e.g., Professor Price in his article of 1938.
[5] Wisdom, "Other Minds", *Proceedings of the Aristotelian Society*, Supplementary Volume (1946). Reprinted in the same volume. p. 193.
[6] "Other Minds", IV.

which one can imagine occurring and which one would feel inclined to call "knowing others in the way one knows oneself". He then forces one gently on to take the next step: "At the moment we reach what we seek it vanishes into something we never sought. You can't have direct knowledge of a feeling, a sensation without having that feeling or sensation."[1] Just as one becomes entitled to call it "knowledge", it is knowledge of oneself and not of somebody else.[2] In other words, "Talk of any other kind of knowing of what is going on in someone else's mind lacks a sense. One who talks of knowing neither by observation of behaviour nor by telepathy of what is going on in the mind of another just doesn't know what he is talking about."[3]

So as the therapy proceeds one begins to relinquish one's insatiable demands for some better, special knowledge of other people which ordinarily one lacks. Philosophically, this is all very heartening, for the lament that we can never really know one another becomes pointless and so loses its sting. In practice we have a good deal of knowledge of other people and can try to improve it. There is no metaphysical block which it makes sense to ask to remove, as we can see when we make a sustained attempt (as Professor Wisdom did in these articles) to envisage its removal. We are not as hopelessly encapsulated as we thought.

Theologically, the position is much less satisfactory. For when the "problem of other minds" is demolished in this way one begins to see, as the dust clears, that a good many Christian presuppositions look like tumbling down also. The theologian in this matter does not find himself exactly on the same side as his non-theological colleague who simply wants to solve the problem: for Christianity on the face of it requires that there should be a problem of other minds. The Christian does not want the philosopher to draw the sting of our finitude by telling us that we know each other adequately already and that in

[1] ibid., p. 100.
[2] See also "The Concept of Mind", *Proceedings of the Aristotelian Society* (1950). Reprinted in the same volume. pp. 227–31.
[3] "Other Minds", IV, p. 97.

any case there could not be any other kind of knowledge of one another of which we could reasonably lament the lack. It is not just a matter of a sort of general policy of the Christian to keep things mysterious, unlike say Professor Ryle who hopes to open everything up to the light of day.[1] It is rather that for the Christian, committed as he is to certain admittedly difficult ways of talking about persons in relationship to one another and to God, Professor Wisdom's cure is like the kind of successful operation of which the patient dies. If "direct knowledge of someone else" is a dream because as soon as it is achieved it turns out that the person one is knowing is oneself, then the pantheist can say "I told you so". To know as I am known is indeed to be absorbed into the infinite. A definite illustration has been given of a proposition already only too plausible: we cannot become one without losing our identities. It seems that all hearts are open now in the only sense in which they could be open, a humanist sense which leaves nothing unfulfilled for Christianity to promise. The whole concept of "unity in plurality" seems more difficult than ever.

It is a great but unconstructive temptation for the Christian philosopher at this stage to dig in his toes, hold on tight to his traditional picture of persons as fortified castles with inner lives which it is possible but difficult to get at, refuse the therapy and put up with the acute inconveniences of an analogical theory of our knowledge of one another. But if he is prepared to go on thinking he will find that his position is first weaker still and then gradually much more encouraging than he has yet had reason to hope.

So far he has only given attention to one strand in Professor Wisdom's analysis. All he began by asking for was a straightforward foolproof account of how we know one another, how we bridge the barriers that are presumed to exist between us; with if possible a thorough knock-down argument against the solipsist. Instead of this satisfaction he has been made to doubt whether the barriers really exist at all. Now it is time for him to realise that the real enemy is not an imaginary solipsist

[1] See below, pp. 133-4.

but a not quite imaginary Behaviourist, that is, someone who holds that the whole "inner-outer" model of a human being is mistaken.

Solipsism as such always was a chimera. Nobody could really suppose, still less argue, that he was all alone in the world, though the supposition has often seemed to need to be argued against. It did on the other hand almost seem possible, in the heyday of logical positivism, to suppose that other people's "inner lives" could be identified with their outward behaviour and so rendered manageable. Such a paradoxical thesis found brilliant though (in its advocate's own words) harsh[1] expression in A. J. Ayer's *Language Truth and Logic*. Without having carried complete conviction, perhaps no more than plain Solipsism ever did, this short way with the "other minds" problem has remained to haunt philosophers, to be refuted or repudiated but never completely quietened. The idea that to say that other people have experiences "means no more" than to say that they will *behave* in certain ways has been so to speak waiting in ambush to catch those who fail to dissolve the problem as Solipsism used to be for those who failed to solve it.

For this anxiety too Professor Wisdom offered a therapy in the shape of a patient investigation into what one is really asking. Is one really "registering a doubt",[2] when one asks whether other people have any "experiences" behind their behaviour? "Is he in pain or shamming?" is a practical question. Perhaps we shall catch him out one day. But it leads on to whole ranges of pseudo-practical questions: "Does he ever feel anything?" "Does he see the Union Jack in red, white and blue?" "Is there *really* an electric current in the wire?" "Do flowers feel?" "Is my watch driven by a brownie or a leprechaun?" What we are supposed to do is resolve our "anxious doubt" into "cheerful indecision", by wondering, as it were, how to award a prize,[3] rather than how

---

[1] *Language Truth and Logic* (1936). Preface to the second edition (1946), p. 5.
[2] "Other Minds", p. 36.
[3] ibid., p. 19.

to answer a question. Of course it takes a long time and a great deal of discussion to make us happy in this way, and some will still feel bound to " 'look down that lonely road' which leads past abandoned illusions to the security of Solipsism".[1] Professor Wisdom lets the speakers in his dialogues have their heads for many pages on the persistent dilemma, that either "Smith will feel sick" means for me, but not for Smith, only his behaviour; or alternatively that I also *expect for Smith*, not for myself, a feeling of sickness, in which case I can never really know whether I have been deceived in him all along.

A later article[2] conducts the analysis more briskly and with more decision. Of course the new model for our knowledge of one another, "We know a man's angry like we know a kettle's boiling"[3] is "too simple". "Anger is more than the pattern of physical incidents which others observe when a creature's angry."[4] Yet the new model brings out the faults of the old one, the house we cannot enter. Just as we are puzzled, but not too puzzled, when someone scratches his head and we are told to do "the same",[5] so with the puzzles about our knowledge of one another we must "keep control of the notations and use or refuse the paradoxes without harm and at our convenience".[6] "No harm is done if we are careful."[7] One model is not expected to be perfect while all the rest are wrong, because "these things" have "a logic all their own".[8]

If in the end the patient is still tempted to cling to his pathological anxiety about other minds, if he still needs the importance of feeling that he is an interesting case and that he might after all still need a theologian as well as a therapist, the physician does not abandon him. He allows that his doubts still have a point, that the

---

[1] ibid., p. 131.
[2] "Other Minds", *Proceedings of the Aristotelian Society* (1946). Reprinted in the same volume.
[3] ibid., p. 195.
[4] ibid., p. 193.
[5] ibid., p. 205.
[6] ibid., p. 206. See above, p. 47.
[7] ibid., p. 213.
[8] ibid., p. 200.

problem of other minds has a "deepest meaning".[1]
Having begun his discussion with a quotation from
Proust,[2] he ends with Virginia Woolf[3] wondering whether
I can ever "know, share, be certain?" She asks if I am
"doomed all my days to write letters, send voices, which
fall upon the tea-table, fade upon the passage, making
appointments, while life dwindles, to come and dine?
Yet letters are venerable: and the telephone valiant,
for the journey is a lonely one, and if bound together
by notes and telephones we went in company, perhaps –
who knows? – we might talk by the way." Falling in
with this mood, Professor Wisdom adds, "This isolation
which we may defeat but cannot vanquish, does it find
voice in the old puzzle as to whether we really know
what is in the mind of others? Does the contradiction
in the philosopher's request for perfect knowledge of
others reflect a conflict in the human heart which dreads
and yet demands the otherness of others?"

When this has been said, can the Christian thinker
ask more? He has come to the philosopher wanting to
clarify his thinking about persons and their relationships,
and he has stirred up a hornet's nest of philosophical
doubts. Is our knowledge of one another really indirect,
or by some mysterious intuition? Does it make any sense
to say that it might have been more direct than in
practice it is? Is there really anything over and above
people's behaviour which one could expect to get to
know? Here are the philosophers being made happy
by the suggestion that they can be satisfied as they are,
with perhaps a wistful glance at the human condition
to give piquancy to their contentment. Can the theologian hope to relax with them, or is he in danger of
quietly losing sight of the Christian concept of a person?

What ought to make him alert and even a little
suspicious, quite apart from his theology, is the generalis-
ing "we" which offers to bind everyone in one bundle
in the very acknowledgment of human isolation.[4] It

[1] ibid., p. 216.
[2] ibid., p. 192.
[3] ibid., p. 217. *Jacob's Room*, p. 91.
[4] I learnt from Michael Foster in his article in *Faith and Logic* " 'We' in
modern philosophy" always to ask who "we" are supposed to be.

would be an unfair overstatement to say absolutely that the problem of human separation is being trivialised, but there is the flavour of a mood indulged rather than of a situation examined. Suddenly the thought forces itself upon one that what is wrong with the proposed answer is not that it is false but that it is enervating. The disease which imprisons each of us within his own self may be diagnosed but it certainly is not cured. The therapist is suffering from it himself, a fact which gives him insight into the condition, but renders him at the same time incapable of finally dispelling it. The offered therapy consists largely of help in facing and accepting the disability. People are mysterious: yes; but this is bound to be so. We cannot reach their inner lives but we must not lament because there is nothing which would count as reaching them. We must learn to feel the doubt and possibly let it deepen our characters, but not to worry about it.

Suppose another response suggests itself instead: a sort of flinging off the bedclothes, a refusal of the medicine. All at once it becomes apparent that for instance in the Virginia Woolf quotation one rather specialised and sophisticated way of looking at human relationships is being taken as typical, so that the manifold varietes of unities and disunities, presences and absences, which human beings establish or undergo in the world of real activity are subtly discounted. This pausing and doubting among the teacups is only a kind of shadow problem of communication. Real problems are different. When people quarrel, when parents are puzzled by their children, when committees produce majority and minority reports on matters of urgent concern, when a close relative is in hospital far away and news is scrappy and conflicting: in these situations one is much more sure, not less, that other people are real.

Seize on to the certainty, then, and begin with that, instead of trying to arrive at the certainty or do without it by devious philosophical methods. This means that one must think in terms of preventing the disease rather than of curing it, or even of learning to live with it; of avoiding the impossibilities of bringing encapsulated persons into relationship with each other, by never letting them be taken apart at all. The exploration of the problem of other minds, has shown one some ways not to go, and so is at last able to suggest a positive way to take. It has put one in a position to see what is needed simply on the human level for the most elementary understanding of persons, if one is not to run into insuperable difficulties. This is a concept of a single world in which persons are already in relationship with one another, in which relationships are already part of one's given data, not something to be tacked on to people afterwards when the argument has advanced far enough. People do indeed have "inner lives", but it is more true to say that they find themselves social and develop introspection, than to say that they find themselves introspectively and develop socially. When this way of looking at the world of persons has been explored a little one should then be in a better position to understand what can be said about the relationship of human persons and God.

CHAPTER NINE

One World

The present task is to consider theoretically the hypothesis which we are all already acting upon practically: the hypothesis that there are many persons living in one public world, interacting with one another in ways which are sometimes simple, sometimes complex; that communication is more basic to human beings than failure to communicate; that privacy is an achievement not an elementary condition. There has in the last twenty-five years been a grand philosophical recovery of this understanding.[1] The "Other Minds" problem has not exactly been abolished, but it has completely changed its terms of reference.[2]

The most elegant and authoritative banishment of the problem was Professor Ryle's *The Concept of Mind*, which might be described as a sustained and largely successful attempt to secure the benefits of Behaviourism without its inconveniences. We are not to suppose that we have special knowledge of our own minds ("privileged access") or that other minds are "occult" entities which we can only approach by strange intuitive leaps or devious and unsatisfactory inferences. We know people, ourselves and others, in quite straightforward ways, though sometimes we get into more or less predictable difficulties in understanding. People are not ghosts inhabiting machines. Sometimes they are open, sometimes mysterious, to

[1] It is also fair to say that it has never been wholly lost. See, e.g., F. D. Maurice, *Social Morality* quoted in *Recovery Starts Within* (ed. Wand), p. 108, (Oxford, 1949), for a fine attack on the view of mankind as "a multitude of units"; and John Baillie, *Our Knowledge of God*, p. 215, for a notable anticipation of Professor Ryle.

[2] It is instructive to compare what Professor Price wrote about the "other minds" problem in *Thinking and Experience* (Hutchinson 1953), pp. 242–3, with his earlier articles. See above p. 120.

themselves or to each other, but this need not be counted as a philosophical "problem of other minds". The refreshing quality of the breath of fresh air which all this let into a space which was becoming increasingly stuffy with philosophical prejudice needed to be experienced to be fully appreciated.

But surely, argues the slowly-departing prejudice, there is a difference between knowledge of oneself and knowledge of others? People know what they themselves think and feel, while for others they have to rely on what they are told and on guesswork? Professor Ryle would insist that in the standard case this is just not so: "In making sense of what you say, . . . I am not inferring to the workings of your mind, I am following them."[1] It is true that I do not read your unuttered thoughts; but I do not read my own thoughts, I think them. One way of thinking them is to utter them, and keeping them to ourselves is something we have to learn to do.

Likewise I do not "know" my own feelings as if they were flashed upon some inner screen accessible only to me: I *have* various twinges, aches and tickles, and know *about* them. You cannot have mine any more than Poland can have Bulgaria's history,[2] but you too can know about them. If this is Behaviourism, it is Behaviourism of a peaceful and unaggressive kind. It does not deny that there are "experiences" over and above "behaviour", or that people have "inner lives", only that this need constitute a philosophical problem. "The world of human experience is in principle and principally a shared world."[3]

Such a theory promises to make suitable allowance both for the ease and for the difficulty of our knowledge of one another, and for the ways in which such knowledge can be both "direct" and "indirect". Of course concealment and even deceit are possibilities; but they are not as it were on a level with openness, for they become

---

[1] *The Concept of Mind*, p. 61.
[2] ibid., p. 209.
[3] Harvey, "An Objective Order", *Proceedings of the Aristotelian Society*, Supplementary Volume (1955), p. 12.

possible just because openness is the norm.[1] One's thoughts do not start as private processes which have to be translated into public language.[2] Ordinarily, one speaks as one thinks, and indeed learning to speak one's own language is part of learning to think. That is why much learning of foreign languages is so inadequate: it is merely learning to translate. If Professor Ryle were wrong, all our speech would be like this.

It must be allowed that in *The Concept of Mind* the case was overstated: it had to be, to make an impression upon the accumulation of generations of overstatement on the other side. People are often deeper, more devious or more inarticulate than John Doe or Richard Roe, and the world is a mysterious place as well as an open place. The point is that if we treat it as fundamentally open we can allow for its remaining mysteriousness, whereas if we treat it as fundamentally mysterious its apparent openness will have to be the greatest mystery of all.

If Professor Ryle's briskness still has a little of the air of a *tour de force*, his goal of a straightforward understanding of our knowledge of one another can be approached by a converging route. Professor Findlay in *Values and Intentions* makes use of the illuminating phrase, "a space of persons".[3] What is needed for present purposes is to envisage such a space, an "auditorium" as he also calls it, as populated by individuals who together take their places in it, who are never initially confined each to his own private interior television screen.

If anyone were so confined he could never get out. It is not just a matter of how the lonely mind could discover that it was not alone and get in touch with its fellows, but of how it could discover that it was lonely. The world would be a unity, experience would have one centre, and this could seem a satisfactorily tidy fact, not a refutable hypothesis.[4] If ever this "solipsism"

---

[1] See R. L. Caldwell, "Pretence", *Mind* (1968). "Vows" (Appendix by Hugh Montefiore and Helen Oppenheimer to *Marriage, Divorce and the Church*), pp. 139–40.

[2] See Ayer in *Studies in Communication*, pp. 20, 23, (Secker & Warburg, 1955).

[3] p. 71.

[4] cf. John Baillie, *Our Knowledge of God*, p. 210.

were abandoned, its rejection would at least be a trau-
matic experience, of which assuredly some trace would
remain, if not in one's own memory, at least in the
visible progress of babies one watched growing up.
However the "human predicament" may properly be
characterised, it is not normally in terms of a real struggle
with solipsism.

Nor is it an irrelevance to insist on looking at the
way in which human beings do in fact develop. It used
to be fashionable to make, and overstate, a distinction
between the way in which we have actually achieved
our knowledge of one another and its philosophical
justification or lack of justification. But the question of
how we know other minds is the question of what we
know them as, and to postulate an entirely imaginary
procedure, valid or invalid, for finding out that one is
not alone in the world has never been a sensible exercise.
It makes more sense to go straight to psychologists,
mothers and nurses, and ask questions about what is
known of the infant's developing self-consciousness; upon
which it becomes abundantly clear that growth to
maturity is a matter of growth *in*, not just towards,
relationships. Lack of relationship is a break, a depriva-
tion, not a natural starting point.[1] There is no plausibility,
either in psychological books or in one's actual acquaintanceship with babies and young children, in any picture
of an infant solipsist surveying the world around him
and gradually acquiring the idea, which one hopes he
will eventually be able to substantiate, that he is
surrounded by other beings like himself.

To start with, they are not like himself. Baby and
mother, in the "consciousness" of the baby, must be
almost entirely unlike, as it were correlative rather than
analogical concepts. What happens is not that he finds
out of his own accord that she is a person like himself,
but that she and all the human beings in his world
teach him through the whole pressure of daily experience
that he is to become a person like them.[2] To learn a
lesson is much easier than to make a discovery; and the

[1] Bowlby, *Child Care and the Growth of Love*, (Penguin Books, 1953).
[2] cf. S. Shoemaker, *Self-Knowledge and Self-Identity*, p. 250.

lesson to be learnt is not the improbable "we are like you" but the gradually verifiable, "One day you will be like us". From the outset one belongs to humankind, and if all goes well self-awareness and awareness of others proceed in tandem.

It has been claimed[1] that thought along these lines makes nonsense of the whole "other minds" problem from the outset and for ever. It seems though less presumptuous to allow that although the sophisticated may concern themselves with it at a later stage,[2] its sting has been drawn as a fundamental threat. People are not essentially encapsulated, although it does not follow that they are immune from ever becoming or seeming to become so. They do not have to find their way from outside into the world of relationship: they start in it and grow in it. "No man is an island, entire of itself."

The significance of all this is by no means as negative as it may have appeared so far. It does not only remove a difficulty in the way of our understanding human beings: it is part of a whole movement towards a positively fuller and more lively comprehension of them, which is the more impressive since it includes thinkers who are by no means like-minded in other ways, It is being realised on all hands that the shrinkage of the concept of a person into a more or less passive experiencer, a sort of wireless receiving set, with all the problems such a view entails about how relationship could ever be established, is in no way demanded by the facts and indeed seriously distorts them.

Among the philosophers Professor Ryle with his insistence that we live in one public world, and Professor Strawson[3] with his somewhat different presentation of the idea of a person as a "primitive" concept including both body and consciousness, both as it were put one in the mood for such a revived understanding of personality as involving relationship. Professor Hampshire's *Thought*

---

[1] e.g., by Norman Malcolm, "Knowledge of Other Minds" printed in *Essays in Philosophical Psychology*, p. 373.

[2] R. L. Phillips, *Philosophy* (1967), p. 114.

N. P. Tanburn, *Mind* (1963).

Don Locke, *Myself and Others*, (Oxford, 1968).

[3] See above, p. 30.

and Action more explicitly makes the point that personal
identity requires the idea of activity, of doing something,[1] not just having experiences possibly quite unrelated
to the experience of other people: "We are in the world,
as bodies among bodies, not only as observers but as
active experimenters."[2] "From the experience of action
also arises that idea of the unity of mind and body,
which has been distorted by philosophers when they
think of persons only as passive observers and not as
self-willed agents."[3] Solipsism as a philosophical doctrine
cannot even be stated, for "My assurance of my own
position in the world, and my knowledge of other things,
develops in this communication and could not conceivably
develop except in this social context. To learn to speak
and understand a language, as a child, is to enter into
a set of social relationships."[4] Only in such an inter-
change can I learn to think about even my own actions.

This movement of thought from person to personal
relationship is entirely possible and natural when the
person is thought of in this way as primarily an agent
not just a knower; it is almost impossible if persons are
imagined as enclosed within their own experience from
the start. The whole argument has been classically set
out by a thinker in a somewhat different tradition:
Professor John Macmurray, in two volumes of Gifford
lectures whose very titles are a summary of the matter,
for they are called *The Self as Agent* and *Persons in Relation*.
The former is a sustained attack, polemical at times
but exceedingly telling, on the "theoretical and egocentric"[5] point of view of traditional philosophy: people are
not just thinkers but doers. The latter is an account,
psychological, philosophical and eventually theological,
of how "we need one another to be ourselves".[6]

A third entirely different approach to what is essentially
the same destination is to be found in John V. Taylor's
fascinating and inspiring book on African religion in

[1] *Thought and Action*, e.g., p. 75.
[2] ibid., p. 53.
[3] ibid., p. 74.
[4] ibid., p. 89.
[5] *The Self as Agent*, p. 11, (Faber, 1957).
[6] *Person in Relation*, p. 211, (Faber, 1961).

relation to Christianity, *The Primal Vision*. "Any attempt to look upon the world through African eyes", he explains,[1] "must involve this adventure of the imagination whereby we abandon our image of a man whose complex identity is encased within the shell of his physical being, and allow ourselves instead to envisage a centrifugal selfhood, equally complex, interpermeating other selves in a relationship in which subject and object are no longer distinguishable. 'I think, therefore I am' is replaced by 'I participate, therefore I am'." To those trained in more analytical ways of thinking such a project might seem dangerously imprecise and obscure, were it not backed by a thoroughly specific account of what this amounts to in African understanding, and by practical suggestions of what it could mean for Christians in the recovery of aspects of their faith which they have long undervalued. It is also worth noticing how surprisingly neatly the point was anticipated by C. C. J. Webb:[2] "we know other minds than our own, not by apprehending them as objects, but through participating with them in a common activity".

A still more theological application of the same fundamental idea has been made by Professor Dodd in two articles on the Immortality of Man.[3] He places the concept of eternal life firmly and fully into the context of the communion of saints, going so far as to assert that human personality "is constituted out of personal relations",[4] so that the idea of heaven makes sense not primarily in terms of individuals but in terms of community. People are right in attaching importance to the hope of meeting again those they have loved and lost;[5] and likewise the social nature of personality allows an answer to the intractable problem of undeveloped souls[6] who can reach their perfection by participating in that society which "lives within the love of God".[7]

[1] *The Primal Vision*, pp. 49–50, (S.C.M., cheap edition, 1965).
[2] *Divine Personaltiy and Human Life*, pp. 203–4, (Allen & Unwin, 1920).
[3] Printed in *New Testament Studies*. (Manchester University Press, 1953).
[4] "Eternal Life", *New Testament Studies*, p. 145.
[5] ibid., p. 146.
[6] ibid., p. 157f.
[7] ibid., p. 158.

The upshot of these various but converging lines of thought is that human beings are not as it were like gingerbread men stamped out, made individual by what divides them from one another. They are more like the knots in the string which makes a net,[1] though this image while allowing for their inter-relationship does not yet make any allowance for their diversity. They are made what they are by their relationships with one another; but "what they are" may become extremely variegated. There is intended no belittling of individuality, rather the contrary, for it is seen as a special achievement not a sort of preliminary allocation.

The ancient theme of man's solitariness in the face of reality, whether as a threat or as an ennoblement, is not made irrelevant: the present emphasis is a corrective to it, not a repudiation of it. Theologians and creative writers who have expatiated upon the theme of estrangement[2] have not been talking nonsense. One can enter imaginatively into the situation of Celia in *The Cocktail Party*:

'. . . It isn't that I *want* to be alone,
But that everyone's alone – or so it seems to me.
They make noises, and think they are talking to each other;
They make faces, and think they understand each other.
And I'm sure that they don't.'[3]

Likewise one is not debarred from appreciating a great individualist like Jeremiah, or from comprehending St. Augustine's wish to die alone,[4] or the desire of men and women to leave the world and become hermits. The point is that none of these is, as it were, a primary situation. They have their poignancy or their nobility in contrast to a common world in which openness is more ordinary than inscrutability.

[1] I have tried to apply this analogy to moral theology in *The Character of Christian Morality*, p. 65.
[2] cf. Tillich, *Systematic Theology* I, p. 186.
[3] T. S. Eliot, *The Cocktail Party*, Act II, p. 124, (Faber, 1950).
[4] Peter Brown, *Augustine of Hippo*, p 432.

Nor on the other hand need there be any suggestion of what is often called a "group mind". Whether the idea is a reputable one or not,[1] it is not involved in the present picture of human life as a network of personal relationships. To say that people are largely constituted by their relationships does not mean that they are so to speak dissolved in them, any more than the knobbly knots in a mesh are dissolved into the string. What is being claimed is that it is fundamentally by interaction with one another and with the material world that human beings achieve their characteristic identity. There is no question at the moment of any blending or melting of that identity into some larger whole in which the individual would be lost. Whatever kinds of unity may eventually turn out to be possible,[2] it is plurality which is here under discussion, and the point is that plurality need not entail the isolation of wholly separate items. The reality of the individual is not impugned but enhanced by an understanding of his nature, on the lines mapped out in Professor Macmurray's two books, as *active* and *social*[3] rather than as passive and solitary. One is not treading what Professor H. D. Lewis has called "the dangerous path that leads all too easily to idealistic monism, if not to pantheism".[4] For the present one has a different, though not necessarily safer, way to tread.

For the shift to the active and social puts the emphasis on will rather than on intellect in understanding the concept of personality. A fundamental concept is the idea of *concern*, a sort of master key which can unlock a great deal of packed-up meaning. One can think of persons in a much more three-dimensional and less diagrammatic way than some philosophers have been wont to do, as living significant lives, not just as having experiences like so many sensitive photographic plates, or pushing each other about like billiard balls. An alternative

---

[1] Professor Strawson hinted, in a somewhat detached way, at its respectability (*Individuals*, p. 113): to the horror of Professor H. D. Lewis, *Proceedings of the Aristotelian Society* (1962–3), p. 21.

[2] cf. p. 168 below.

[3] See above, p. 138.

[4] *Journal of Theological Studies* (1964), p. 234. in a review of John Baillie, *The Sense of the Presence of God*, (Oxford, 1962).

142   INCARNATION AND IMMANENCE

keyword could be the notion of "care",[1] more explicitly
warm and human than "concern", but for that very
reason to be used more warily for fear of assuming too
much. Either word can, but need not, suggest a faint
twinge of anxiety, sometimes apt enough as a way of
justly characterising human life. Whichever concept is
used, when this fuller meaning ascribed to the individual
in his relationships is looked at critically it will prove
as alarming to some as any suggestion of a group mind
could be, for what now seems liable to be confused is not
the distinctness of separate persons but the distinctness
of fact and value.

On the one hand, to characterise personal *activity* in
terms of concern means that one has to think of this
activity not as merely mechanical but as purposive.
At once for better or worse one has left plain fact behind
in favour of something more elusive. Purposes are
satisfied or not satisfied, harmonious or the reverse,
and their various compatibilities and incompatibilities
add up to happy or unhappy human lives. The gap
between fact and value here, from the satisfying to the
satisfactory, is enticingly narrow, even narrower than
the famous gap between the desired and the desirable,
and it is very attractive to attempt the forbidden jump
from the "is" to the "ought". One is in the perilous but
important region of the proper ends of man.

Similarly in the context of the notion of "concern"
the concept of the *social* is almost impossible to keep
neutral. Talk of human beings as essentially beings-in-
relation, and therefore of personal relationships as a
fundamental aspect of human life is apt to have a strongly-
marked moral flavour; but why should it not? The subject
matter of morality is after all human living, and it is
this value-laden character of human affairs that the
word "concern" is useful in bringing out. One must be
philosophically careful here but not defeatist.

Ethical presumption is as great a danger here as
philosophical ineptitude: one needs to keep a certain

---

[1] cf. Bertocci, "The Person God is" in *Talk of God*, p. 187, (Macmillan,
1969). "Any *person* is the kind of being who is a knowing-willing-caring unity
in continuity."

austerity, a resistance to sentimentality, in what one means by a personal relationship, if the whole discussion is not to become insufferably woolly. Professor Dorothy Emmet has put in a wise caution about maintaining a "positive respect for what is rightly impersonal", without which "our relations with other people can degenerate emotionally".[1]

The essential point is that a person is not a lone disinterested thinker but a being who "matters" to himself and to other people. One can neither eliminate this idea of "mattering" from the concept of a person, nor eliminate all moral content from the idea of "mattering". Brunner goes so far as to say "the idea of value only has meaning at all in relation to a person".[2] Be that as it may, the present argument is really the converse, that the idea of a person only has meaning in some relation to value, via this concept of concern. This is where David Jenkins takes his stand at the beginning of *The Glory of Man*,[3] and the issue could not be more clearly put:

> I assume that our concern is with persons. If it is not, then I assert that our concern *ought* to be with persons. To refuse or ignore this concern is a failure to face up to what is involved in being a human being. To reject a concern with persons which is commensurate with the concern which persons as such demand is a refusal to face facts which amounts to a fundamental error of judgment about value. It is also a rejection of value, an attitude of immorality, which flies in the face of recognisable facts. People who refuse a proper concern for persons are immoral as human beings and wrong as judges of matters of fact.

In other words, a moral dimension has now been brought in, and deliberately brought in, to fill out the elusive concept of immanence and help to establish its

---

[1] *Journal of Theological Studies* (1962), p. 235, in a review of Macmurray's second book.

[2] *The Divine Imperative*, p. 195, (Lutterworth Press, English translation, 1937).

[3] *The Glory of Man*, pp. 2–3.

significance. This is not to suggest that immanence is a moral term, *instead* of being a metaphysical term, but rather that it has possibilities of being meaningfully metaphysical because it has to do with what human life is about: it need not be thinly abstract and theoretical. Persons, that is, cannot be described fully without the understanding that they *matter* to themselves and to others, and it is in this mattering that the possibility of their unity-in-plurality resides. To "abide in" one another comes to look as if it could be a human reality and not just a theological fancy. It remains to go on and apply this "non-deistic" picture of persons as capable of relationship to the relationships they do form, particularly those which are the subject-matter of theology.

IMMANENCE, HUMAN AND DIVINE

CHAPTER TEN

Grace Impinging

The last two chapters have been inspired by a passage written by Ian Crombie in *Faith and Logic* as long ago as 1957.[1] If we are to believe Christian doctrine, he says

> we must so conceive of human nature that we can find room in it for the possibility of the spiritual presence of Christ. What we are to find room for is still of course positively an unknown; but negatively we know something about it – we can think of many things which it would be meaningless mystification to describe in this way. This may be enough to set us looking; it may, for example, be enough to suggest that our conception of human personality is too flat or two-dimensional to fit any such notion to it. Thus we may come to reform our conception of human personality; and it may be that, having done so, we find that we now have a better understanding of what men are, even apart from the strictly religious context. With our deepened conception of human personality may come a hint of an inkling of what spiritual presence might be.

Now that a little of this theoretical spadework has been attempted, it is time to return to the doctrine of divine immanence to see whether it has indeed been at all opened up, whether the rejection of what might be called the "gingerbread men" or "cake-cutter" view[2] of

---

[1] "The Possibility of Theological Statements", *Faith and Logic*, p. 75. H. R. Macintosh impressively used a similar argument over sixty years ago in *The Person of Jesus Christ*, pp. 338–9, (T. & T. Clark, second edition, 1913). What I have called the "cake-cutter" view of human personality he calls the "adamantine" view.

[2] See above, p. 140.

human personality helps to render less obscure the manner of God's presence to human beings. It is an attractive supposition that one may learn more about God's grace within one from comparison and contrast with the interplay of human relationships than from theoretical divinity; that human dependence and independence, maturity and immaturity, control and release, and especially human concern, might provide valid and even authoritative illustrations of creaturely relationships with God.

But first it needs to be insisted that the operative word is "interplay" and that the human relationships are in the plural. Religious thinkers have been so much impressed and enlightened by Martin Buber's simple and profound division of personal relationships into just two kinds, "I – Thou" and "I – It" that it is in danger of becoming a shibboleth. It seems needful to point out, rather ungraciously, that in some contexts the contrast could operate as an over-simplification.

To speak the "primary word" *I – Thou* and so to take one's stand in relation[1] rather than to make another person an object, an "It", is an admirable, indeed an exciting concept which on the one hand answers to a great deal in one's real experience and on the other suggests a happy continuity between deep relationships with each other and relationships with God. "Man receives, and he receives not a specific 'content' but a Presence, a Presence as power."[2] The difficulty is not that human life does not rise to such heights. There is no doubt that people do find the idea of "I – Thou relationship" a valid and illuminating way of understanding their experience. The trouble is that in its penetrating simplicity it interprets the known more effectively than it guides one into the unknown. For those who are still looking for data to interpret, who are still uncertain whether the Emperor really has anything on, it could mislead by its very incisiveness. For anyone who is over-anxious to find an I – Thou relationship with God it could be a serious temptation to make sweeping

[1] *I and Thou*, p. 4, (T. & T. Clark, 1936).
[2] ibid., p. 110.

and premature applications of the *Thou* versus *It* distinction to human life.

Curiously enough the result of such an uncritical application of the contrast is not to elevate human relationships unrealistically on to too high a plane, but to belittle most of them. "It" in English is too tidily the word for a thing in complete distinction from a person to be able without distortion to include in its scope all that is not "Thou", all You and He and She. As Professor H. D. Lewis has pointed out, one does not relegate even the most casual passer-by to the status of a mere It: "I should be frozen with horror if a car seemed about to run him down."[1] Maybe the case is different, less cut-and-dried, in a language such as German where *things* have gender, but if one is thinking in English it is essential to remember that plenty of valid and valuable relationships are liable to be ignored or even diminished if only "I – Thou" is allowed to count for anything. Dr. Harvey Cox has shed a flood of useful light on the more complex possibilities of the real human situation.[2]

Nor is it adequate just to acknowledge that "I – Thou relationships" can be a matter of degree. It is too easy, if one is thinking theoretically about persons rather than practically about human beings, to fall into the habit of putting all kinds of relationships which deserve the name at all on to one scale ranging from enemies through neighbours to nearest and dearest, the only differences being quantitative, how loving or unloving. But both logically and humanly it is an impoverishment to lump together and assimilate every available relationship, brother and sister, husband and wife, shopkeeper and old customer, strangers smiling at the same joke or helping in the same emergency, teacher and pupil, competitors in an open tournament,

---

[1] "God and Mystery", *Prospect for Metaphysics*, ed. I. T. Ramsey, p. 214, (Allen & Unwin, 1961), cf. Paton, *The Modern Predicament*, p. 167, (Allen & Unwin, 1955).

[2] *The Secular City*, pp. 40–9, (S.C.M., 1966 edition). cf. Edward Carpenter, "Integrity in Thought and Life", *Christ for Us To-day*, ed. Norman Pittenger, p. 190, (S.C.M., 1968). It can be instructive to look at a sociological account of variegated relationships such as Willmott and Young, *Family and Class in a London Suburb*, (Routledge & Kegan Paul, 1960).

colleagues on a committee, motorists in collision, next-door neighbours, childhood friends. To which of these the concept of "I – Thou relationship" applies is not and ought not to be made to seem a simple question. The warning is especially needed if one hopes to use human relationships as one finds them to illuminate the high relationships of theology: relations between man and God, the Father and Christ, the Spirit and the Church. The "non-deistic" picture of human life which encourages one to look afresh at the doctrine of God's presence in terms of interrelationship between persons is essentially a complicated picture, not a simple and schematic one.

The Christian doctrine of grace, of how God impinges upon human beings as it were from within, is certainly in need of any constructive illustration which human life and experience can provide. It can be stated sympathetically in such a way that the believer is not being simple-minded when he allows himself to be encouraged and carried along by it; but it remains a sufficiently difficult and paradoxical doctrine that, conversely, there need be no perversity or cold-hearted infidelity in being puzzled or even baffled by it. A good example of an authoritative and attractive but not necessarily wholly self-justifying statement of it can be found in Professor Burnaby's *Amor Dei*:[1]

> Grace not only respects, but intensifies and enlarges our freedom. The "help" of grace means no division of labour: it does not mean that part of the work is ours, and part God's. Cardinal Bellarmine wrote that "in the good work which we do by God's help, there is nothing of ours that is not God's, nor anything of God's that is not ours. God does the *whole* and man does the *whole*." That is genuinely Augustinian.

For many, and particularly for those Christians who know at first hand in their own lives[2] what Professor Burnaby is talking about, here is a statement of the

---

[1] p. 239. His reference to Bellarmine is to *De Justificatione*, v. 5.
[2] cf. Farmer, *The World and God*, p. 101.

matter in which they can contentedly rest: but for some
it remains only a constructive statement of the problem.
More teasing remarks will churn about with it: H. R.
Macintosh's confident "No man has ever complained
that Jesus' will misled him",[1] or Professor Hepburn's
rueful "Remove the paradox from 'Work out your own
salvation . . . For it is God which worketh in you' and
much more is lost than economy and beauty of expression".[2] More particularly, a frontal attack reviving
traditional difficulties[3] has quite recently been made
upon the whole traditional concept of God's grace as
entering into man's will, a thoroughly responsible and
not even unsympathetic attack which deserves a like
responsible consideration.[4]

Professor Maclagan, the protagonist in this matter,
is no hostile atheist or glib sceptic. In his profound and
subtle book *The Theological Frontier of Ethics* he shows
himself thoroughly conversant with the world of Christian
theological thinking and by no means an alien in that
world.[5] He is very well aware that the doctrine of grace
is "an integral part of Christian theology", but feels
obliged to ask urgently "whether it is a doctrine that
can and, given its truth, should be incorporated in our
account of the moral response, or whether it is on the
contrary incompatible with any account that would
be ethically satisfactory".[6] His conclusion is blunt:[7]

Now there is nothing at all to be gained by any beating
about the bush in this matter. Even at the risk of
seeming to deal cavalierly with a great issue, of seeming
content to proffer the stone of crude assertion where
what is asked for is the bread of satisfying argument,
I must make what is in the end a simple point with

---

[1] *The Person of Jesus Christ*, p. 328.
[2] "Poetry and Religious Belief", *Metaphysical Beliefs*, pp. 152–3, (S.C.M.,
1957).
[3] See above, p. 49.
[4] I have broached the subject briefly in an Appendix to the report *Marriage,
Divorce and the Church*, p. 127.
[5] e.g., pp. 108–10, (Allen & Unwin, 1961).
[6] p. 110.
[7] p. 111.

simple and emphatic directness. As regards the self-regulation of the will when faced with a moral challenge, the sheer "making up one's mind" and "setting oneself" to do what seems required of us, not only is there no observable presence – I cannot conceive how there could be – of any power not our own operating within our will, but to suppose that in some unobserved way such a power is in fact operative is to suppose something that is in contradiction with the very idea of a free willing.[1]

This line of thought amounts to a serious and indeed explicit[2] "new Pelagianism", not to be brushed aside on the ground that Augustine settled these questions centuries ago. Nor is anyone who thinks in this way a facile optimist under-estimating man's sin and need for grace. What is being denied is that the concept of grace as actually entering into man's own will makes sense. Professor Maclagan draws an essential distinction between what he calls "environmental" and "constitutive" grace.[3] Environmental grace is help from outside, however close and important to us. Constitutive grace would be grace propelling us from within, and it is only this which he is disposed to deny. He expatiates movingly upon grace as entering into our "most intimate environment"[4] but insists that the will itself must be our very own. When a child enters for a painting competition[5] and his entry must be "all his own work" we are well aware of the ways in which his parents may and may not help him. If he wins the competition he may say "I could never have done it without them"; he may even say something like St. Paul's "I, but not I"; but the emphasis will be upon the first "I". Were it not,

[1] See also Professor H. D. Lewis, *Our Experience of God*, p. 270, (Allen & Unwin, 1959). Professor G. F. Woods stated the moral difficulty succinctly and left his readers with it at the end of *A Defence of Theological Ethics*, p. 130, (Cambridge, 1966): "I know of no theory of divine grace which is not open to moral criticism. The Gospel always remains a mystery to the Law."

[2] Maclagan, p. 107–8.

[3] p. 115.

[4] p. 126.

[5] pp. 114–15.

he would have lost his integrity. In the same way, Professor Maclagan would insist, the moral life must be "all our own work". Even perfection can be expected of us,[1] but we must achieve it for ourselves. He is willing to take the full consequences of this severe theory, that "the ideal condition of the will" is theoretically within our powers; though certainly a man "need not be astonished even if . . . it has never yet been fulfilled or, perhaps he would wish to say, has been so only once".[2]

However chancy one may consider this Christology, Professor Maclagan's ethics are far from being lightweight. It is not possible here to do justice to the range and depth of his discussion of the highest morality in terms of a religious response, but it has a notable warmth about it: there is no coldly legal conception of "paid in full". His argument requires to be taken seriously, and its whole tendency is to cast fresh doubt on the Christian concept of unity-in-plurality: it certainly begins again to look as if separate persons cannot become "one" in any strong sense without abandoning their identities, ceasing not only to be separate but to be persons.

Professor Maclagan is so eminently reasonable and unprejudiced, allowing all he can to his opponents at each point, that there are moments when the issue begins to seem fine-spun almost to vanishing point; but what is at stake is the whole Christian doctrine of Immanence. It does make a fundamental difference in the end whether we may say, "not I alone but also God in me" or only "I not of myself but only by God's help".[3] For Professor Maclagan personal influence, whether human or divine, can never amount to anything which could properly be called Immanence except merely figuratively, or else, deplorably, in terms of hypnotism.[4]

His courteous and exacting argument has made it impossible smoothly to by-pass the difficulty and re-propound the traditional view. He has ruled out of court the bland assertion that Immanence just is the

[1] pp. 105–6, 120f.
[2] p. 124.
[3] p. 114.
[4] p. 116.

way God differs from people, that because He is God He
can enter into our very wills whereas we cannot enter
into one another's except "environmentally". With
such a premature expedient, Professor Maclagan will
rightly have nothing to do. If there is to be an answer,
it must be by way of a different understanding of personality as such, so that either one can apply what one
wants to say to human beings as well as to God, or at
least one can see some reason for making the distinction
other than the sheer difficulty of the whole topic. Such
an understanding must somehow be more flexible than
Professor Maclagan's without becoming intellectually
shoddy. It is only with trepidation that one can attempt
such an answer at all, where evidently Oman's great
book *Grace and Personality* has been weighed in the balance
and found wanting.[1] Simply to bring back the standard
human analogies, parent/child, husband/wife, pupil/
teacher, when it is plain that Professor Maclagan has
considered and rejected them would be what he calls
a "blank counter-assertion",[2] not a piece of argument.
But still it must be said, with all diffidence, that there
is a rigidity in Professor Maclagan's account of personal
relationships, which though in welcome contrast to the
sentimentality which sometimes prevails, is perhaps
not the last word.

Or rather, Professor Maclagan is not primarily seeking
to give an account of personal relationships as such at
all. What he is concerned with is the individual moral
agent and his ultimate autonomy, his ability to choose
the right which is the one thing worth while. Seen from
this point of view the individual choice must in the last
resort be able to operate untampered with by any
influences, beneficial or sinister, external or internal.
If either scientific law or the doctrine of grace impugn
this final freedom, then so much the worse for scientific
law or the doctrine of grace:[3] morality itself must be
ready to do battle on this issue. The scientific determinist
indeed may not worry too much about this hostility,

[1] pp. 115–16.
[2] p. 112.
[3] See above, p. 49.

for he is not necessarily concerned to defend morality in Professor Maclagan's high Kantian sense, and can take the field merrily against the libertarian, not caring about this particular casualty. The believer in grace on the contrary cannot really be happy to defend his position with the loss of either morality or, in the end, of logic, and so he has to reckon with the strength of Professor Maclagan's arguments at an early stage. His hopeful empirical illustrations about the influence of parents upon children as attempts to show the compatibility of grace and freewill seem to crumble in the face of the moral and logical argument that responsibility must be mine and nobody else's if morality is to mean anything.

It is easy enough for the believer in grace to forget at this stage why he is fighting this battle at all. He, like Professor Maclagan, has a specific moral position to insist upon and therefore may turn out to be less vulnerable to the argument that grace is ultimately incompatible with morality than might at first appear. His arguments about parents influencing children need not be just defensive "oh but surely" arguments, quickly succumbing to the inexorable need for a moral agent to be autonomous. Rather, when properly considered, they are themselves part of an alternative but equally moral insistence on the need for a moral agent to be a person in relation to other persons, not a being in a vacuum.

In other words, Immanence is not a doctrine which Christianity just happens to be saddled with: it is an aspect of Christianity which is convincing because it is empirically and morally congruous with a way of looking at the nature of persons which is credible in its own right. The position at which the previous chapter arrived, that people need each other to be themselves and that "mattering" is a fundamental aspect of what it is to be a person, is not necessarily incompatible with Professor Maclagan's insistence on the autonomous "bare will"; but its suggestion that "mattering" involves impinging upon one another in a more profound way than the merely external is at least a very different emphasis, arrived at by an entirely distinct but no less respectable route.

The Christian has as much right to take this emphasis seriously as to accept Professor Maclagan's and no right to brush either aside. It cannot be very satisfactory just to set these two concepts of a moral agent alongside each other like waves and particles, even though that is what Professor Maclagan himself is eventually constrained to do, albeit reluctantly, with his personal and impersonal concepts of the nature of God.[1] It would be better either to show the "bare will" view as inadequate compared with the "persons-in-relation" view, or to show that they are not incompatible with one another in the end.

To achieve either of these aims it is fair to begin by meeting Professor Maclagan at the key point he insists upon, the bare human will at its simplest and most uncluttered, and to go along as far as possible with his argument. Suppose then that this is indeed the ultimate and correct refinement of one's understanding of a moral agent, this frail and seemingly vulnerable but wholly autonomous chooser, liable to be blown about on every wind but unable finally to abdicate responsibility, for it holds its status not even by divine right but by inescapable logic. Only when a real effort has been made to see the matter in this way can one begin to be sure that there is something missing. To repudiate this rarified conception is not to seize on to a hopeful debating point but to try to do more justice to reality

Professor Maclagan himself has given part of the answer, in allowing that his "bare will" is an abstraction from "everything else that goes to make up our personal life".[2] He admits that some people may not be disposed to care very much when this "abstract discarnate little wraith" is denied the inward presence of God's grace;[3] though he goes on to argue persuasively that far from being a vicious or a trivial abstraction it is a needful one. Certainly the concession he has made does not amount to enough on its own to save a recognisable doctrine of Immanence. On the contrary, it leaves all influence upon the will firmly outside the will itself.

[1] p. 179.
[2] p. 126.
[3] ibid.

Disarmingly Professor Maclagan makes the very point his opponents might have thought to make against him: that his argument "relates to a mere figment, a sort of mathematical point in the spiritual world, spoken of as though it had magnitude".[1] In his terms and according to his view of a moral agent, he can well afford to make this concession. But if one's concept of a person as a moral agent is based not primarily on the idea of individual responsibility but on the idea of a being that matters to itself and others, one has got somehow to go beyond abstractions. The point is that this is as *moral* a requirement as the requirement of unimpaired freedom. Without cancelling the demands of freedom, maybe without even doing justice to them, the emphasis on relationship sets up the rival claim that a moral agent is not finally to be shrunk to an extensionless point. It is not only that such a point is abstract, as Professor Maclagan allows. It is also in an important way *static*. A choosing person can be said characteristically to gather momentum, whatever implications this fact has for the freedom of the will. The "bare will", on the contrary, confronted with choice after choice, must apparently be a new entity each time. In so far as it is "bare" it is abstracted not only from its own environment but from its own past.

The mention of the past gives a hint of a possibly far-fetched way of trying to resolve the difficulty. Professor Ryle in *The Concept of Mind* was as dissatisfied with the traditional doctrine of self-knowledge as Professor Maclagan is with the traditional doctrine of grace. It may be fanciful to suggest that there is a similarity about the two problems:[2] in each case one becomes involved in a kind of illegitimate reflexiveness, an attempt to find in the very being of the "self" something which it seems to need yet which blocks it from being itself. Self-knowledge seems to get between us and ourselves in something like the way in which grace seems to get

[1] ibid.
[2] Perhaps less fanciful if one remembers that in Berkeley's *Alciphron* (7th Dialogue) "myself" and "grace" are both treated as "notions": words which "may be significant although they do not stand for ideas".

between us and ourselves. Perhaps a similar answer may help for both.

When we know what we are doing, Professor Ryle asks,[1] does our attention fluctuate between our "selves" and our doings? To deny self-knowledge "seems to reduce my knowing self to a theoretically infertile mystery" while to affirm it "seems to reduce the fishing net to one of the fishes which it itself catches".[2] The suggested answer is that the problems which arise from looking on "introspection" as a kind of self-illuminating interior process[3] can be solved if we think of ourselves as looking *back* on our own doings in immediate retrospection, not confusingly "within".[4] He explains the concept of a "higher-order act",[5] an act which is directed upon another act, and which can in turn have acts of a yet higher order directed upon it. To detect, report, copy or mock, are examples of such actions;[6] for example I may report (third order) that she mocked (second order) my attempt to sing. My more or less successful efforts to scrutinise my *own* conduct or motives are not different in kind. The process of moving from first to second-order act can be almost instantaneous, but so long as it is not quite instantaneous we do not have to talk about strangely phosphorescent inner processes[7] which could only impede themselves. If self-knowledge can be accounted for in this way there is no need to say that an act of knowing must either know itself or remain forever unknown, any more than a record in a diary records itself or an argument criticises itself.[8] Yet acts can all be known, immediately or later, just as records can presently be recorded and arguments criticised.

The object of this discussion has been to suggest that maybe it is not necessary after all for the personalist to insist in a way in which Professor Maclagan would

[1] *The Concept of Mind,* pp. 164–5.
[2] p. 187.
[3] p. 159.
[4] pp. 166–7.
[5] p. 191ff.
[6] p. 192.
[7] p. 159.
[8] p. 196.

disapprove, that one act can gather up in itself both freedom and grace. As a free decision, whatever that means, the act is wholly autonomous, but the person who makes the free decision has become what he is by taking into himself over the years the influences of all kinds, human and divine, which have formed him for better or worse. What has been in question is in what sense if any the free will can be said to be influenced, and the point is that the distinction between "environmental" and "constitutive" influence shrinks to vanishing point when it is shifted even a very short way into the past. What has been my environment is always in process of becoming part of myself: my home, my family, my friends, and if so then why not my God? By all means insist that at the abstract moment of choice I must act entirely for myself in logical solitariness. Allow next, as Professor Maclagan does, that I can be accompanied to the very brink though not across it by the help of others. What needs to be added now is that what I am at any particular brink may be effectively formed, up to though still not across that brink, by the influence of others. In making a choice I muster all that I am, so that the plunge I take is my own at the moment of making it but has not been all my own. The mathematical point to which Professor Maclagan's argument reduces my bare will is always something more significant than a point on its own; it is rather the apex of a large and complex figure, and it is this figure, not the mathematical point, in which the personalist is practically and theoretically interested.

The personalist will want to say that it is part of being human to build one's environment into one's very self, so as somehow to form part of that ongoing thrust which characterises a real person. He will be inclined to say that people make one another; but at the very least he will insist that they give one another impetus. He will refuse to go back to that "cake-cutter" picture of personal existence which he has been particularly concerned to reject. Without necessarily denying the whole concept of the "bare will", he will look on it as so to speak the spearhead of his existence, not as all there is of him.

In other words, like Professor Maclagan the personalist
"must make what is in the end a simple point with simple
and emphatic directness".[1] The bare will may be a
needful and legitimate abstraction, but it is not an
entity which either I or my friends can recognise as
"me". I am more than my bare will and the "more"
is compounded of influences and inter-connections,
wholly impossible to disentangle, but essential data for
anyone who wants to understand persons. To put the
matter more bluntly still: to insist upon the distinction
between "environmental" and "constitutive" influence
may safeguard responsibility but it drives a wedge into
relationship, which cannot in the last resort be treated as
something merely external, even at a human level.
The issue has been neatly expressed in one sentence,[2]
worth quoting because it so to speak "moves the closure":
"Everything that is not I is 'outside' myself". The personalist has to insist that the logical simplicity of this is not
true to the complexity of human moral existence.

Were he just to stop here, he could well be accused
of mere mystification. He must have something positive
to say about relationship as he understands it, and about
the sense in which he believes that people can impinge
upon one another. In what sense, he must ask, can one
person "enter into" another person's will? If one is
talking about "the will" as an entity that chooses and
must not be interfered with in so doing, one will want to
say "not at all", and one can claim to have common
sense on one's side. "Wills will not splice and dovetail
like deal boards",[3] said Bentham. But put the emphasis
differently and talk about the will as an entity that
chooses, and there is more to be said. Choice presupposes
purposes: and one can certainly enter into another
person's purposes. Emphasise this aspect of a person
still further, and look on the idea of having purposes,

[1] Maclagan, p. 111. Quoted above, pp. 151–2.
[2] By Mr. Fielding Clarke in his attack on *Honest to God*, called *For Christ's Sake*, p. 18, (Religious Education Press, 1963).
[3] *A Fragment on Government*, ch. IV, 10. Quoted by Dorothy Emmet, "On 'Doing what is right' and 'Doing the will of God' ", *Religious Studies*, Vol. 3 (1967–8), p. 293.

of being disposed to make choices, as integral to the very
notion of a personal being.

It is this emphasis which is brought out when the
concept of *concern* is used as a keyword,[1] and one comes
to define or at any rate characterise a "person" in terms
of "having concern". Next comes the tautology that
it is by way of one's concern, that is by way of what
matters to one, that one is capable of being impinged
upon by others. It then follows that the more "concern"
is allowed to mean here, the more "impinge" can come
to mean also. Suppose, to push this view to the limit,
that it is the nature of a person to be a sort of bundle
of concerns, as some philosophers used to think in terms
of a bundle of sense-impressions. Then it would even
be true to say that to unite one's concern with another's
would literally be to unite one's self. Possibilities open
up of talking about unity of will with one another and
with God on the lines of unity of concern rather than
of any kind of mystical absorption. "We cannot touch
God," said Austin Farrer, "except by willing the will
of God."[2]

What is important though if anything is to be made
of "concern" as a key notion in this manner, is not so
much to push this theory to the limit as a philosophical
account of personality, as to be sure to use the word
"concern" itself in a strong enough sense to bear the
weight which is being put upon it. It needs to be understood in a stronger sense than it usually carries, almost
a technical sense, to mean not just an interest, anxiety
or affection but, so to say, what a person is really "up
to", what his existence is about: so that a shared concern
really does mean something like a shared will or a
shared life. The Quaker use of the concept, if I understand it correctly, suggests something of what is required
here: or the Hebraic way of using the word "heart".
"Oh knit my heart unto thee, that I may fear thy name",
said the Psalmist.[3] To use, and stretch, a metaphor, one
might call concern the "spring" of the will, meaning

[1] See above, p. 141.
[2] *A Science of God?*, p. 107.
[3] Psalm 86.

11

not its "source" as if it were a stream but something more like the "mainspring" of a clock, "what makes it tick". The caution is of course badly needed at this point that to talk about "the will" as an entity at all is already dangerously metaphorical. The excuse for taking the risk must be that there are things one wants to say about persons which can best be said in such language.

Without some such interpretation of "concern", to explain unity of will in terms of it would be to reduce the whole concept to no more than mere co-operativeness, at a cost of trivialising one's understanding of human life and morality. Certainly one would not get very far in using the idea of unity of concern to explain unity with God, if by this one could indicate no more than a sort of "democratic notion of partnership".[1] We are supposed to be "fellow workers with God", but we do not co-operate with Him for common objectives. But one way of expressing this very thought that we can never be equal partners with God is to say that His ways are not our ways and His thoughts are not our thoughts. In other words, one is talking of God's concern even while insisting that finite creatures cannot fully enter into them. And on the other hand in so far as we can hope to have dealings with Him it is as a personal God with concern for His creation; and this indeed is what both the Old and the New Testaments are about. Likewise to affirm that He has dealings with us is to say that we also, made in His image, are personal beings whose concerns somehow lay us open to His grace.

The claim which is being made is that it is by virtue of having *concern* that personal beings can and characteristically do impinge upon one another in such a way that the language of independence becomes inadequate while the language of absorption remains irrelevant. Surely, it may be said, there is still a fatal asymmetry here: we cannot say that we impinge upon God. Our wills enter into His by conforming, His into ours by

[1] I am grateful to Professor Dorothy Emmet for this criticism of my notion of "unity of concern", in correspondence and in "On 'Doing what is right' and 'Doing the will of God'," *Religious Studies*, Vol. 3 (1967–8), p. 293.

enabling. This is true but can easily be overstated. In a sense it can after all be said that human creatures do impinge upon their Creator; or what can be meant by for instance the Collect for the first Sunday after Trinity, which asks precisely for the help of God's grace that we may *please* Him, both in will and deed? Whatever divine impassibility means it is not intended to rule out God's delight in His creation; nor has it ruled out in Christian thinking His capacity to suffer for the sake of its fulfilment. Concern in the sense in which the word is being used here has something to do with both delight and vulnerability.

It is not to be presumed that all this argumentation has done more than nibble at the great classic problem of grace and freewill. Its aim has not been the overweening one of solving the problem, but rather of clarifying its conditions: of insisting that a will that can be impinged upon is as necessary a datum for understanding personal relatedness, as a "bare will" that cannot is for understanding human responsibility. The matter can be brought to a head by giving, so to speak, one more push to the notion of concern. As developed here it has turned out to be practically synonymous with the notion of *love*. In effect, what is being maintained is that the "bare will" offers no purchase upon which love can take hold, and is therefore a non-starter as the sole vehicle of moral personality.

Of course this last statement is highly controversial. It is often held and preached that real love, divine love and human love as it ought to be, does precisely love a person just as essential person and not for any accidental embellishments. "Only God, my dear, can love you for yourself alone and not your yellow hair." Enormous questions open up which demand a study to themselves.[1] For the present it is enough to point out that whether or not the bare will can be loved, the object of introducing the bare will into the argument was to take the will *out* of relationship to consider it wholly in itself; and to the emphasis of this programme in the last resort the personalist will have to object. He will instead reiterate

[1] And which will be touched on later (pp. 184ff).

that if there is to be any purpose in trying to understand persons at all it must be persons as we know them: and persons as we know them are not adequately characterised except in inextricable relationship to one another. The mention of "love" was not a sentimental red herring, a setting of heart against head, but, for the personalist, the explicit claim to moral relevance which makes him dare to oppose his point of view even to one so weighty as Professor Maclagan's. It was a shorthand way of making the point that relationships not only exist, they "matter", they are morally significant; and therefore of declining any ultimate abstraction which has to leave them out.

CHAPTER ELEVEN

Unity-in-Plurality

To have announced at an earlier stage in the argument
that love is the key to the problem of grace would have
been merely pretentiously platitudinous, but now it
may be hoped that such a statement can begin to take
on a more precise meaning. More accurately though less
ambitiously, it is being claimed that the way to illuminate
the Christian theme of "personal immanence"[1] is by
developing a full and not too schematic a picture of
persons in relationship; and that along this line one can
hope to understand better how we can be said to be
"one with" God and each other without losing our
separate identities. What has been arrived at is not yet
any account of the Immanence of *God* but the suggestion
that some kind of immanence is a characteristic of
persons as such, that human beings themselves cannot
be accounted for in the clear-cut way which comes
naturally to the deist. In opposition to the principle
that "Everything that is not I is 'outside' myself"[2] may
be set a definition by Professor Dodd[3] which can serve
partly as a summary of what has already been said,
and partly as a signpost from which to move on: "Love
is that relation between persons in which alone perfect
social unity co-exists with the utmost freedom of the
individual; for only where love is, can two or more
persons be completely themselves while transcending
their separateness in a common life."

What distinguishes such a statement from the sort
of "blank counter-assertion"[4] deplored by Professor

---

[1] See above, p. 107ff.
[2] Quoted above, p. 160.
[3] *New Testament Studies*, p. 155.
[4] Maclagan, p. 112, quoted above, p. 154.

Maclagan is, in the last resort, only its intrinsic convincingness. One just has to ask oneself whether indeed love among human beings is after all like this. If human "immanence" is eventually to shed light upon theology, human "immanence" must be findable in its own right. It must preferably be something one wants to talk about anyway, whether one has any theological preconceptions or not. There must be occasions when people want to speak within the plain limits of human life of unity-in-plurality: of two becoming one while still remaining two, where neither is absorbed nor swamped by the other and yet neither can properly be treated as an independent being confronting the other as part of the external world.

The time has come for definite assertion that such unity-in-plurality is in fact a fully recognisable human phenonemon. One knows what it means to talk about such relationships, and if there is paradox in such talk it is not impertinent paradox. A close relationship between two human beings, as experienced, can amount to a unity which is not at all like some sort of mystical absorption on the one hand nor on the other like a human counterpart of deism.

Theologians are possibly not the best people to refer to here, for it will inevitably be suspected that they have an axe to grind: that they are still indicating what for theological purposes they need to find, rather than considering human life for its own sake to see what they do find. Some of them though have put the matter so clearly that it would be a pity to rule them out of court. Bishop Newbigin spoke of "the paradox of which all know something who know what love is – the mutual losing of isolated self-hood to find it in the beloved",[1] and Vincent Taylor of "a union which is not the loss of identity but the enrichment of life".[2] Again, the test of such assertions must be whether the situation of which they speak is indeed recognisable. A more unselfconscious

---

[1] *The Household of God*, p. 125, (S.C.M., 1953).

[2] *Jesus and His Sacrifice*, p. 311, (Macmillan, 1951). See also e.g., Kemp, *Man Fa'len and Free*, p. 170, (Hodder and Stoughton, 1969). Quick, *Essays in Orthodoxy*, p. 168, (Macmillan, 1916), N. P. Williams, *The Grace of God*, p. 124, (Hodder and Stoughton, 1966).

illustration can be found in *Great Expectations*,[1] where something like the concept of "personal immanence" is used not as any kind of philosophical or theological argument but simply as a way of describing a situation admittedly fictional but not far-fetched:

> It was not because I was faithful [says Pip], but because Joe was faithful, that I never ran away and went for a soldier or a sailor. It was not because I had a strong sense of the virtue of industry, but because Joe had a strong sense of the virtue of industry, that I worked with tolerable zeal against the grain. It is not possible to know how far the influence of any amiable honest-hearted duty-doing man flies out into the world; but it is very possible to know how it has touched one's-self in going by, and I know right well that any good that intermixed itself with my apprenticeship came of plain contented Joe not of restless aspiring discontented me.

Such examples are of course no substitute for a closer look at the concept they seek to illustrate. They are part of a rather gradual approach to it; and even so, to confine one's attention to them could be like travelling through foothills without ever happening to look up at the high peaks beyond. Human immanence has all this time a prophet whom it would be ungrateful to ignore: Pierre Teilhard de Chardin, with his resounding slogan *Union differentiates*. His elaborations upon this theme could be described as the superb grinding of an axe. For all that he is writing as a scientist, he is certainly not sitting down quietly and patiently to be instructed by the facts, but gives rather the impression of conscripting the facts to serve his dream; but it is a great dream and by no means an insubstantial one. It is nothing less than this, that the next stage of human evolution is now due and is to be the joining of our separate personalities into a super-personality with no loss but rather enrichment of our individuality. With characteristic enthusiasm and

[1] Chapter XIV.

eloquence he expresses it like this:[1] "Hence we have the following formula for the supreme goal towards which human energy is tending: an organic plurality the elements of which find the consummation of their own personality in a paroxysm of mutual union and limpidity: the whole body being supported by the unifying influence of a *distinct centre* of super-personality."

Surely this is recognisable as the same dream which inspires the passage in the Epistle to the Ephesians: "till we all come in the unity of the faith, and of the knowledge of the Son of God, unto a perfect man, unto the measure of the stature of the fulness of Christ".[2] His preoccupation with evolution is not just a somewhat pathetic determination to drag modern science into Christianity somehow, but is entirely of a piece with the Pauline conception of the whole creation travailing together[3] towards deliverance. His works might well be read as an extended sermon on that text in Ephesians about the fulness of him who filleth all in all.[4]

The traditionalist may well prefer the biblical way of putting it, but if he finds that Teilhard's approach is indeed having some success in casting out the twentieth century devil of lack of interest in Christian formulation, then he is not to forbid him. What is to the present purpose is the theory, or call it rather vision, of human immanence which backs up the dream, and to get the flavour of it it is worth attempting to overcome one's analytically-trained alarm at a passage like the following:[5] "A convergent world, whatever sacrifice of freedom it may seem to demand of us, is the only one which can preserve the dignity and the aspirations of the living being. Therefore, *it must be true.*" He does go on to explain what he means, with arguments drawn from the cell-structure of higher forms of life, from animal association, from human societies and from personal relationships: "In every practical sphere *true union* (that is to say,

[1] *Human Energy*, pp. 144–5, (Collins, 1969).
[2] Ephesians 4: 13. (A.V.).
[3] Romans 8: 22.
[4] Ephesians 1: 23. See also Colossians 1: 17–20 (3: 14–15).
[5] *The Future of Man*, p. 54, (Fontana, 1969).

synthesis) does not confound; *it differentiates*".[1] He enlarges upon this in an essay called "Sketch for a Personalist Universe":[2]

> This is the truth. Not only *a priori*, that is to say by deducing the future of the world from a property which conditioned its past; but *a posteriori* by observing around us the creative effects of love, we are led to accept this paradoxical proposition, which contains the final secret of life; true union does not fuse the elements it brings together, by mutual fertilisation and adaptation it gives them a renewal of vitality. It is egoism that hardens and neutralizes the human stuff. *Union differentiates*.[3]

Now if one is at all in sympathy with all this it is invigorating and even inspiring; but it is necessary to be clear about the role it can play in the present argument. Teilhard is not offering, and should not in fairness be criticised as if he were offering, a dispassionate analysis of the human situation. He is offering a goal to be achieved, a "grand option", and the function which argument performs in the presentation of his case is to persuade us that the goal can be achieved and that there are tendencies now operative to encourage us to believe that it will be achieved. He is indeed preaching a sermon, albeit a rational sermon, not studying a concept. In so far as he is successful he will touch off new ways of living, not just explain life as it is.

If on the other hand one is trying to study a concept, there is no need to repudiate the sermon nor even necessarily to look upon it with suspicion; but we must still look on it critically, and ask questions about its validity. Has one the right to be invigorated and inspired by Teilhard de Chardin's vision? And, more particularly, has he contributed more than a sort of exciting incantation to the present problem? Certainly one has reservations,

---

[1] ibid., p. 55.

[2] Published in *Human Energy*.

[3] p. 63. See also "The Phenomenon of Spirituality" in the same volume (pp. 103–4) for a very characteristic exposition of these ideas.

based on doubts about how we are to recognise the
arrival of his consummation in distinction from its non-
arrival, doubts about why it is supposed to be due
particularly now rather than in more evident connection
with the events of the Incarnation, and doubts about
his general attitude towards the problem of evil. But with
these reservations one can still affirm that Teilhard is
expressing fundamentally Christian aspirations in a
powerful way which at least some people are finding
constructive and suitable for our day; though it is fair
to say that he has done more for the recovery of such
aspirations than for their elucidation. Coming at a time
when people were understandably afraid of the collective,
his writings have borne witness that they need not
likewise be afraid of unity and openness, that on the
contrary unity and openness are what mankind needs
and can be what mankind will attain.

The present theme is much more prosaic: to attempt
to probe further into the meaning of the concepts of
unity and openness in their Christian and sometimes
technical forms. The reason for bringing in Teilhard
de Chardin has been that his slogan *Union differentiates*,
expounded as he expounds it, has a truth and a vividness
which makes it a good pointer in the pursuit of the
concept of personal immanence. It must be admitted
that anyway one reader of Teilhard has made use of
the signpost the other way round. An existing preoccupation with personal immanence and the discovery of this
eloquent expression of it served to overcome a suspicion
of Teilhard's whole manner of approach. Expressions
like "union of concentration"[1] or "the meeting *centre
to centre* of human units"[2] seemed less opaque than they
might otherwise have done because they seemed to
fit with the notion of "unity of concern" and to make
sense in association with it. It does not seem impossible
then that conversely there may be some for whom
Teilhard's rather mighty witness may help to overcome
suspicion of the concept of personal immanence.

Yet the best witness must be convincing illustration;

[1] *Human Energy*, p. 104.
[2] *The Future of Man*, p. 78.

and there is one particularly obvious and indeed favourite example which comes to mind: the relationship of marriage. The ground here is so well-trodden that it can be with no sense of dénouement that one eventually arrives at this point, but the example is a particularly promising one none the less, and it is worth while to specify why.

To begin with, it meets the requirement already suggested[1] of being a topic much studied in its own right quite apart from theology. If some aspects of marriage considered as a human institution[2] turn out to shed light upon theological thinking, this is less likely to be due to some sleight of hand on the part of the theologian and more likely to be due to what he would ascribe it to, some genuine homogeneity in the character of God's world. But at the same time a Christian will hardly be surprised to find that marriage among human institutions is particularly useful in illustrating the meaning of immanence, when it is already an authoritative image for one kind of immanence, the unity between Christ and his Church.[3] To make use of this example is to associate oneself with traditional Christian thinking, not to ride a hobby horse of one's own. A little care and clarity is needed here lest this reason for looking hopefully upon the marriage illustration should seem to conflict with the first reason. Has the argument not swung rather suddenly from marriage as a secular institution to marriage as a Christian sacrament? On the contrary, this swing, far from being required by the argument, would for the present be positively unhelpful to it. When it was first affirmed that the union between man and wife signifies to us the union between Christ and his Church, it was assuredly the secular human institution, not "Christian marriage" as developed for nineteen centuries, which furnished the human side of the analogy. Had both sides been theological from the beginning the illustration could not have got started.

---

[1] See above, p. 166.

[2] *Marriage, Divorce and the Church* (the Report of the Commission on the Christian Doctrine of Marriage), paragraph 46ff.

[3] Ephesians 5: 31–2.

The complication is that even already in the Epistle to the Ephesians the illumination is going both ways. The union between Christ and his Church is immediately, even primarily, shedding light back upon marriage, which is to become a new thing by no means untouched by theology: to the enhancement of human life but also to the possible confusion of theologians.

The point remains that however Christian one's understanding of marriage may become, the institution of marriage which is to be understood has its basis in the order of creation rather than the order of redemption.[1] Taken as such it has been available as an important image for divine realities. What concerns the present argument is that one way in which marriage is qualified to be such an image is by its character as a vivid example of the notion of immanence in fully human terms, before any theological applications begin to be made. This last affirmation cries out to be substantiated, and it may be substantiated by being made more specific still. It is not just any characteristic of marriage or even any characteristic of a good marriage which is to the purpose here, but certain particular characteristics of a somewhat prosaic kind. The point on which the argument needs to fasten is that among human relationships marriage illustrates the notion of immanence with special effectiveness because in marriage the two aspects of unity and plurality which are required are both at their clearest. One could easily lose this point in lofty expatiations on the height and intensity of love which human beings are capable of feeling for one another. This would be hardly at all to the purpose. What is needed is something much smaller in scale, a sharper focussing which can be achieved better by something as plain and cool as legal definition. In English law marriage is "the union of one man with one woman, voluntarily entered into for life"; and here precisely is the notion of unity-in-plurality. It is legally, not just poetically, that a married couple may be treated for some purposes as one person. They are evidently in some senses still two entities: there is no confusion here; but they are not two separate

---

[1] Genesis 1: 27. *Marriage, Divorce and the Church*, paragraph 49.

entities. Their association has a reality such that even in the eyes of the law the whole is greater than the sum of its parts. It is not an ordinary contract which may be brought to an end at the mere will of the parties, but a "contract conferring status" which requires the intervention of a court for its dissolution.[1]

Nor are these aspects of marriage legal fictions. They correspond to common-sense realities. Make all needful allowance for human diversity and it remains true that in society as we know it it is an entirely ordinary state of affairs for the bond between husband and wife to enhance not destroy their individuality; for both "dependence" and "independence" to be necessary ways of characterising their relationship; for something like the terminology of grace and freedom to be used quite readily without the anxious logic-chopping which has sometimes characterised its more theological applications. One finds it natural not baffling that a husband and wife should feel that they need each other to be fully themselves, and that they should be wholly unable to sort out mathematically what is of one, what is of the other, and what is of both. Whatever they feel for one another, their lives are joined by a common *concern* which makes the word "union" an accurate characterisation of a way of life, not a half-dead cliché. Such a union of concern when fully developed is much more like self-love in its all-pervasiveness and matter-of-factness than most other forms of human affection or devotion. Like self-love, it is neither creditable nor discreditable; it can be calm or tormented; it can be welcoming or hostile towards the outer world.

It may be said that this is all very well but that these considerations are surely somewhat far-fetched. Do they not overlook one plain fact: that it is after all the *physical* union, not some mysterious unity needing discussion in terms of immanence, which primarily differentiates marriage and which has always been intended as the human side of the Christian image? To complicate the

---

[1] The introduction of the word "consent" into the new English divorce law obscures but does not obliterate this significant distinction. See *Putting Asunder*, paragraph 59, (S.P.C.K., 1966).

"one body" theme with all these relational considerations seems to flout common sense, and to risk importing twentieth-century preconceptions into biblical affirmations. To this criticism a two-fold answer may be given. First, if in our century an increased appreciation of the life-sharing and personality-enhancing aspects of marriage[1] proves able to enrich a time-honoured Christian image, so much the better. Secondly, such appreciation does not ignore but needs even to be based upon the fact of physical union, understood not as merely physical but as signifying total commitment.[2] Such an understanding of the meaning of sex in human life is at least not foreign to the biblical emphasis.

This interpretation can apply sacramental theory to marriage in a somewhat different way from that which has been traditional in Catholicism. Instead of saying that marriage is itself one of the sacraments, it suggests rather that sex is to marriage what the sacraments are to Christianity:[3] the physical expression of spiritual reality. With this understanding one is in a position to develop the relational aspects as much as seems appropriate to one's twentieth-century mind, whether in studying marriage or in studying theology, without feeling that one is losing touch with the authentic Christian "one body" theme.

The present purpose is not to discuss marriage as such or even at the moment the union between Christ and his Church, but rather to use marriage as an illustration of the concept of human immanence. As usual, there comes a point when the significance of the illustration can be brought out more fully by contrast. What sort of relationship would *not* be an example of unity-in-plurality? It is not just depth or intensity or even just sincerity of feeling which is being looked for but a certain balance between oneness and otherness which can be conspicuous by its absence as well as by its presence. Catherine's declaration in *Wuthering Heights*, "Nelly, I *am* Heathcliff", in so far as it is not just a fine piece of

---

[1] *Marriage, Divorce and the Church*, ch. II.
[2] ibid., paragraphs 28–31.
[3] ibid., paragraph 31.

hyperbole, is an illustration of a kind of "immanence" which is much more like mystical absorption than the concept under investigation here.

Another negative example may serve to emphasise that the marriage illustration is supposed to be playing a precise and unpretentious role, not a vaguely uplifting one, in the present argument. Take a portrayal of a great love which has an immensity to which few human beings would aspire, but which, to put it mildly, lacks some of the characteristics of an ordinary marriage: Shakespeare's *Antony and Cleopatra*. To call this a negative illustration of the concept of human immanence in the sense of unity-in-plurality is not just to make the obvious and even rather priggish observation that at no stage do the lovers show any fundamental trust in one another; nor even just to reiterate that it is not passionate attachment as such which betokens shared life or shared concern; but rather to characterise the specific unity of marriage a little more distinctly by showing that it cannot be located in just any significant relationship.

Here is portrayed a union which does not "differentiate" but which for Antony at least involves the loss of his characteristic identity. His relationship with Cleopatra has a nobility of its own to which Enobarbus is alive: this is more than the sordid little tale of temptation and fall discussed with relish or regret among the other Romans; but it cannot be said that these lovers enhance each other's individuality or find freedom in their mutual dependence. On the contrary:

> Egypt, thou knew'st too well
> My heart was to thy rudder tied by the strings,
> And thou shouldst tow me after; o'er my spirit
> Thy full supremacy thou knew'st, and that
> Thy beck might from the bidding of the gods
> Command me.[1]

What follows is a kind of disintegration: as pictures seen in the clouds grow "indistinct, as water is in water". Antony feels he cannot "hold this visible shape", and

[1] Act III, scene 9.

with a perceptive but far from astringent self-pity he knows himself to be "no more a soldier".[1]

Yet with a complexity akin to real life the love of Antony is not depicted without elements of life-enhancement, elements, so to say, of human grace, which make it able to yield positive and not only negative illustration of the immanence theme. In particular, Cleopatra's lament at the death of Antony could be, in these terms, the lament of a wife for a husband. The desolation, the loss of vitality, is for more than the extinction of a particular person, it is for the extinction of the world in which that person lived: for the loss after all, not perhaps exactly of a shared life, but of a shared universe in which life had meaning.

> O! withered is the garland of the war,
> The soldier's pole is fall'n; young boys and girls
> Are level now with men; the odds is gone,
> And there is nothing left remarkable
> Beneath the visiting moon.[2]

What is relevant is not the poignancy of the loss but its so to say generalised character. King Lear is heartbroken, literally, at the death of Cordelia, but he gives voice to his grief in sharply individual terms:

> Why should a dog, a horse, a rat, have life
> And thou no breath at all? Thou'lt come no more.[3]

It would be too easy to labour the point,[4] but if the comparison has any validity it does suggest a somewhat unexpected fact: that the relationship between parent and child can be interpreted as another negative illustration rather than automatically as a positive one of the notion of human immanence.

[1] Act IV, scene 12.
[2] Act IV, scene 13.
[3] Act V, scene 3.
[4] There are other Shakespearean examples. Compare the generality of "Othello's occupation gone" (Act III, scene 3, lines 350–7) or Macbeth's past caring "life's but a walking shadow" with the particularity of Troilus' horror at the death of Hector.

Surely such an interpretation must be perverse, when fatherhood is the most highly authorised image of all for the relationship between man and God? It is indeed, but its context is rather the transcendence than the immanence of God. It is a way of understanding that His authority over us, far from being that of a tyrannical monarch, is of a wholly personal kind. In His kingdom we are to be heirs, not frightened subjects. His will is to be obeyed not as arbitrary command but by loving response, and He will bear the cost of it Himself. These contrasts are the answers to different problems from the question about unity and plurality. They assume God's distinctness and seek to resolve its forbiddingness, rather than assuming His closeness and seeking to resolve its threat to swallow us up. To speak in Trinitarian terms, it is with the Spirit that the doctrine of immanence is associated: to try to locate immanence in fatherhood could be a kind of "confounding the persons".

Humanly speaking certainly there is just such a risk in parenthood, and it is worth pointing out, not to moralise but to help exhibit the concept of immanence in action. People tend to expect a great deal of "immanence" between parents and children, with consequent failure of understanding both practical and theoretical. To say this is not just to point out the only too obvious fact that parents are often reluctant to allow their children to grow up, a point which it would be needlessly grandiose to express in terms of immanence. It is rather that some people who are not going to make that mistake are still dominated in their understanding of parenthood by a concept of unity-in-plurality which is more suited to the understanding of marriage: a concept in which the unity and the plurality are kept in balance, rather than a concept which will allow the plurality steadily to prevail. Personal immanence has been neatly expressed as "freedom-in-dependence",[1] and the rearing of a child is not precisely an example of this but of a development from dependence to freedom.

[1] Baelz, *The Phenomenon of Christian Belief*, ed. Lampe, p. 16, (Mowbrays, 1970).

Like marriage, parenthood can be characterised as a spiritual reality based on a physical bond; but it is easy for a parent to underestimate the essentially asymmetrical nature of the physical relationship on which parental love is based, and so to act on, not too high but the wrong kind of expectations of the spiritual reality. The parent is a sort of creator, and knows this with awe: how natural then to go on living through the child's being and make the child a fresh and improved embodiment of one's own self. There can be humility in this, not only pride and possessiveness, but it comes to an end at best in bewilderment and at worst in bitterness as soon as children begin to stamp their own individuality upon their own enterprises. Parents can call down the blessings of heaven upon their children's heads, but they cannot go through their experiences with them. The only right they have in the matter is a sort of right to find this tautology surprising, to hail it as a discovery.

This could be put in Professor Maclagan's terminology by saying that parents of all people have to learn to relinquish the longing to provide their children with "constitutive" grace. This is not because such grace is impossible or illegitimate in itself. Had Professor Maclagan applied the concept of "all my own work" to the marriage relationship for instance, his argument could have been much less telling. It is because immanence does not properly belong to *parenthood*. If this were better understood both humanly and theoretically some Freudian criticism of the Christian attitude to the heavenly Father might become unnecessary. Parents, under God, are the creators of their children and of their children's environment, and what this can mean in loving relationship, which certainly can be called grace, is incalculable: but they are not there to enter into their children's spirits and live in their lives.

The fact of family likeness can mislead here. It is a marvel to see somebody one is fond of remade in his or her offspring, but it is wiser to delight in this as likeness in distinctness than as unity-in-plurality. Here are the same characteristics yet expressed in two separate lives; not, here are two different lives joined in one. A strong

likeness between brothers or sisters could be a safer
illustration of "immanence" than a likeness appearing
in a new generation: particularly in the case of identical
twins, one may sometimes have a lively impression of a
bond so close that one of them really is able to speak
for both. This is exactly what a parent cannot or anyway
ought not to do for a child; which is not to deny either
a seemingly all-inclusive responsibility nor a unique
relationship which need not be impoverished when the
stage of upbringing is outgrown. Such a relationship
at its best in its continuing asymmetry transformed into
independence can become a sort of spontaneous keeping
of the Fifth Commandment, Honour thy father and
thy mother.

Having refused to take this relationship as a good
example of human immanence, one must now proceed
to complicate the picture. First, nothing which has
been said ought to rule out the possibility of forms of
the institution of parenthood in which something like
"immanence" plays a much more significant part.
Mr. John Taylor in *The Primal Vision*[1] quotes a prayer of
the Dinka:

"You of my father, if you are called, then you will
help me and join yourself with my words. . . . And you,
my prayer and you prayer of the long distant past,
prayer of my ancestors, you are spoken now. Meet
together, ee! It is that of my ancestor Guejok, it is not
of the tongue only; it is that of Guejok, not of my tongue
only."[2] This, he argues, is not "ancestor worship" in any
idolatrous sense; it is something much more akin to the
Christian belief in the communion of saints, and the
African experience of human solidarity is not to be
repudiated but brought in to enrich Christian understanding. "The dream of the tug-of-war" (pulling the
African out of his world into the Christian one) "was a
true picture, but neither hand is meant to let go. The
strangers with the crosses in their hands will win in
the end but only by pulling all the old ones from long

[1] See above, pp. 138–9.
[2] *The Primal Vision*, p. 170. Quoted from Godfrey Lienhardt, *Divinity and Experience*, p. 221.

ago into their own realm."[1] Where such a bond between the generations is indeed experienced, then "immanence" is a proper category in which to speak of it; but of course there should be no question, either way, of forcing one pattern of parenthood into the mould of another.

Secondly, by picking out marriage and parenthood from among human relationships and trying to differentiate them so tidily, one could soon begin to get diminishing returns in the enterprise of trying to understand the notion of immanence; for one is losing touch with the route by which one has come. When theological deism began to break down, it was suggested that such breakdown was only to be expected, since the theory of persons as distinct and separate units with which deism operates will not work even for human persons. If something like immanence has got to be reckoned with apart from theology, it will surely eventually be applicable more naturally to theology. But to "reckon with immanence" is not to take just one particularly promising example of it in human life and contrast it so strongly with other cases that one makes it harder, not easier, to find what one is looking for elsewhere. The reason for picking out the clearest example was to follow out the concept of immanence as potentially characteristic of personal life as such. The shape of human relationships is not diagrammatic but consists of an intricacy of diverse forms of concern for one another, through the whole of which the notion of "unity-in-plurality" may hopefully be hunted.

---

[1] *The Primal Vision*, p. 171.

CHAPTER TWELVE

Partiality and Immanence

In the characteristic, not necessarily idealised, relationship
of husband and wife one can see writ large a recurrent
rather than a unique pattern in human life: the possibility
of a sort of balance of independence and dependence,
of giving and taking, of freedom and control. That
people are incomplete without other people, that in
concern for one another they can be united yet remain
distinct, that an individual is hardly a person in his
own right but is formed by other people and what they
mean to him, are plain facts of experience, not theological
distortions of it. For all this the moral word "love" can
be a convenient shorthand, but what it stands for has
relevance not only to the practice but to the theory of
human life.

In other words, one may come to realise that something
like the Christian concept of immanence is not after all
foreign to what people are but on the contrary is integral
to their natures.[1] One begins to indulge the hope that
perhaps this is "what we were made for"; but here is
a place where one could easily start to move much too
fast. It would be tempting enough to suppose that one
had arrived in full view of the theology of immanence
by way of the idea of "concern for one another" when
all one had really done was go for a circular walk like
Alice in looking-glass land, "trying turn after turn, but
always coming back to the house, do as she would".
For where has the *theology* of immanence got to? How has
all this discussion of human inter-relationship helped
in the identification of relationship with God?

The immediate necessity is to make clear what it has
not done. Divine immanence has not been located yet.

---

[1] cf. above pp. 144, 147, 159.

The object of taking heed of human immanence has not been to look closer and closer and then suddenly say "Eureka! In concern for one another we find our ultimate concern. Here is indeed the presence of God." That would be to send the Emperor sunbathing. It would be to find an immanence which is not the correlative of transcendence, a unity without plurality. It would be an easy mistake to make, for it exalts and isolates a characteristically Christian belief, that God is indeed present in our relationship with one another: but what this can mean is the problem, not the answer.

The contribution which "human immanence" is supposed to make, and has gradually been brought to the threshold of making, to the understanding of divine immanence is by way of analogy not assimilation. If "immanence" is not a special theological concept but can have secular uses, the secular can surely help to interpret the theological. But now a new objection arises: the fact that one seems to have proved too much. Why after all did immanence ever look so difficult? If in discussing it one was really only talking about something which is readily to be found in everyday human life, what has become of the problem? The question at the outset was that certain Christian commonplaces about abiding in God and in one another are much more obscure than one could wish: that the affirmations Christians want to make about God's relationships with his creatures are *not* apparently illuminated by ordinary relationships between people as we know them. In such a situation it cannot be much help to reiterate the commonplaces after a sufficiently long discussion that one has lost sight of the beginning, claiming as a great discovery that we can abide in one another and so presumably in God.

It is true though that the mid-twentieth century inherited a philosophical tradition in which the ordinary "immanence" of human life was being more and more overlooked, in which persons were being understood primarily as separate and intellectual entities in such a way as to make the very possibility of relationships between them seem to be mysterious. Philosophers had become so "deistic" about people that it was hard for them to be anything but deistic about God.[1] It has not therefore been unfair to present natural human relatedness as a discovery, or rather as a rediscovery.

But on top of this there could be another reason why Christians in particular have tended to underestimate human immanence so that this cautious exploratory prowl through what ought to be familiar territory has become necessary. There is a sort of would-be reverence which constantly tries to claim for the immediate province of the Almighty aspects of the world which seem on the face of it to have been left, in His wisdom, in human hands. So Christians colonise human life on behalf of God's kingdom and human relationships especially are apt to be taken over in a way which circumscribes rather than enhances their proper character. Human love comes to be regarded as a sort of tolerated aboriginal, scarce and puny, not a self-respecting creature imprinted plainly with God's image.[2] One example of this tendency is the supposition that marriage outside the Church must be a soulless contract; another is that way of thinking which dignifies any social gathering of Christians however trivial by the name of "fellowship"[3] while treating human *friendship* as either unimportant or as a sort of honorary "fellowship", not something in its own right. Simone Weil finely says[4] that "Pure friendship is an image of that original and perfect friendship which belongs to the Trinity and which is the very essence of God", and goes on, "It is impossible for two human beings to be one while scrupulously respecting the distance which separates them, unless God is present in each of them." No doubt she is right: but too hasty a demand for God's *overt* presence if a human relationship is to be counted as valid at all has reduced many Christian

---

[1] See above, p. 117.

[2] See e.g., Brunner, *I believe in the Living God*, p. 136, (Lutterworth Press, translation, 1961).

[3] I have expatiated on this theme in an article in *Theology* (September 1968) called "Head and Members; the Priest and the Community he serves", printed in *The Sacred Ministry*, ed. G. R. Dunstan, (S.P.C.K., 1970).

[4] *Waiting on God*, p. 160, (Fontana, 1959).

pronouncements on these themes to pious emptiness.

When to "abide in one another" is treated as *ex officio* a theological manifestation, one may find that one has simply removed out of human life those aspects of it to which one might have looked for explanation and illumination of what the theologians are trying to say. Where the great traditional images are concerned the relevance of the secular as such is clear enough to see. Human comparisons do not belittle the divine but open up ways of talking intelligibly about it, both by analogy and contrast. "If you then being evil give good gifts to your children, how much more shall your heavenly father . . ." conveys something to people who have experience of fatherhood. "The Church is the Bride of Christ" is significant because marriage is already a secular institution. Even here the temptation to "colonise" the secular is not always resisted. Where one is on relatively fresh ground, where one is ranging at large through the whole diversity of human relationship looking for fruitful comparisons, the danger of not pausing long enough to appreciate what exists before trying to wring theological meaning from it becomes much greater. So if all this discussion can be counted as a sort of purposeful pausing, the claim that the theological problem looks different at the end of it may not appear quite invalid.

But after all, is there not a much greater danger of appreciating human relationships far too much? This whole line of thought has been running more and more in opposition to a great tradition in Christian thought which insists that the concern which joins us to one another is not at all the same kind of thing as the love whereby God loves us. God's love is Agape, the love which gives unconditionally: unredeemed human love on the contrary is essentially based upon selfishness, on grasping need or selective choice, and the kinds of unity which it occasions are wholly unfit to serve as models for supernatural unity. To win back the right to set up human immanence as a clue to divine, something must be done, not presumptuously to attempt to prove the worthiness of human love, but to show that to take it apart from divine love in this way will sooner or later impoverish both. The case can stand being somewhat overstated, not in the hope of destroying the contrary picture completely but to redress the balance which has gone very far the other way.

Much has been written and will no doubt still profitably be written in praise of specifically Christian love, that unwavering goodwill for the other person simply because he is there, which takes no account of any attractive qualities he may have or lack, which asks for no return or reward, which simply is unconditional acceptance. In so far as we can love like this we are entering into the love of Christ who died for us while we were yet sinners, and this is far more worth while than explaining what we are doing. In so far as we take our stand in human love which attaches itself to those it finds pleasing, we are still being selfish.

But, problems of immanence apart, is this quite right? In loving us God is not fulfilling any needs of His own or asking any reward, but surely He is asking for a return, in the sense of response? He accepts us unconditionally as we are now, not so that we can go on being miserable sinners,[1] but so that we may glorify Him and enjoy Him for ever.[2] The enjoying is not supposed to make sense without the glorifying: the wedding guests will be expected to wear wedding garments: and the real question is, would one wish it otherwise? Is wholly self-giving undemanding Agape in the last resort something one wants at all? Many human loves could do with being much more unselfish than they are; but to be loved and have literally nothing asked of one, and to be made to feel that there is no way in which one can ever give back anything of any value, is to be made a pauper.

To show the strength of the contrary position, it is fair to quote from C. S. Lewis:[3] "Thus, depth beneath depth and subtlety within subtlety, there remains some

[1] cf. H. A. Williams, *The True Wilderness*, pp. 132–3, (Constable, 1965).
[2] cf. C. S. Lewis's magnificent essay "The Weight of Glory", published in *They asked for a paper*.
[3] *The Four Loves*, pp. 148–9, (Bles, 1960).

lingering idea of our own, our very own, attractiveness.
It is easy to acknowledge, but almost impossible to
realise for long, that we are mirrors whose brightness,
if we are bright, is wholly derived from the sun that
shines upon us. Surely we must have a little – however
little – native luminosity? Surely we can't be *quite*
creatures?" With respect it may be suggested that what
is in question here is not "native luminosity" but as it
were creaturely luminosity. Granted that we are "*quite*
creatures", we were made to reflect the light, to be at
last lovable as well as loved. The point may seem too
fine, but what is at stake is not the worthiness or unworthi-
ness of human beings but the power of God to make
something ultimately worthwhile or not.

The requirement which mainly serves to drive a
wedge between Christian love and human attachment
and looks like blocking attempted analogies is "unconditional"; but it is a decidedly odd requirement. "We do
not love our neighbour because he is *such* but because he
is there"[1] said Brunner firmly, but when this distinction
is looked at really hard it seems to grow faint. "I accept
you whatever you are like" sounds godlike and "I find
you congenial" self-centred, but it is not a very great
step to convert these into carelessness, "I don't mind
what you are like" on the one hand and appreciation
of a unique person, "There is nobody like you", on the
other, and the whole picture alters. There are good
reasons too for looking at it this way round, for a person
who is "there" but not "such" is a merely abstract
entity, of which any but a merely abstract love must
slide.[2] To resist pure formality as a potential impoverishment and look for something more concrete is not to
make the obstinate and shallow assumption that love
should be a matter of feelings, but rather to allow even
the highest love to have some kind of content, to refuse
to mark it off so sharply from the lower loves which
frankly are concerned with qualities.[3]

Another phrase of Brunner's, "the welcoming of one

[1] *The Divine Imperative*, p. 330, note 1.
[2] See above, p. 163.
[3] See Burnaby, *Amor Dei*, (Hodder and Stoughton, 1938), p. 309.

another in diversity",[1] is a much warmer characterisation
of Christian love than a prohibition of taking individual
characteristics into account; and at the same time it
seems to promise to allow comparison after all between
Agape and human relationships, and even with the most
evidently secular of them all, human friendship. Is it
so very unworthy to value a person for his or her unique
distinctiveness, a potentially life-enhancing flavour which
is special to that person? It is easy enough to belittle
this as a mere attachment to what happens to be congenial,
but it could be far more constructive just to allow the
picture to shift and focus a little before one's eyes and
to realise that this could be to love somebody as made in
the image of God. In other words, instead of loving
regardless of any value, one has ground for trust that the
value is there, and the more one looks at people in this
light the more qualities one can hope to find to delight
in, not in a uniform way, but in creative diversity.
In this way one could make a beginning in appreciating
even the most unpromising person. "The Lord has given
him a mark which ought to be familiar to you";[2] though
here it is being suggested that the mark is likely to be
not uniform but diverse. This case could be overstated
as easily as its opposite and there could come a time
when it would be necessary again to insist that *agape*,
unlike *eros*, "*confers* value" on its object.[3] But in the
meantime a robust piece of argument of Professor Price's
is worth emphasising.[4] "It does not feel like that. It
feels more like discerning than conferring, when its
object is another human being. We are told that love is
blind. So it can be. But it can also open our eyes. It can
reveal good qualities in the loved person which others do
not notice, and even good qualities which are as yet
potential rather than actual."
    Granted all this, and granted in particular that among

---

    [1] *The Letter to the Romans; a commentary*, p. 120, (Lutterworth Press,
translation, 1959).
    [2] Calvin, *Institutes* III, vii, printed in Beach & Niebuhr, *Christian Ethics*,
p. 286, (Ronald Press Co., New York, 1955).
    [3] e.g., R. W. Sleeper, "On Believing", *Religious Studies* (1967), Vo. 2,
p. 83.
    [4] H. H. Price, "A reply to Professor R. W. Sleeper", ibid. p. 243-4.

the diversity of human relationships human friendship
with its appreciation of the individual is after all not an
unworthy model of divine love: this still does not make
it necessarily relevant to the present specific problem,
the better understanding of those supernatural relationships of unity-in-plurality which come under the heading
of "immanence". On the contrary, it seems to be
characteristic of friendship that the people concerned
are not exactly united but remain alongside one another.[1]
It would seem that there cannot be much illumination
by analogy to be found here, and that attempts to
establish a contrast could be so readily successful as to
amount to very little. It is supposed to mean something
to say that we dwell in Christ and he in us: this is plainly
not what happens in friendship: so the only result of
bringing friendship into the case at all could be to make
us discontented by making us realise just how intangible
and obscure our relationship to Christ and to each other
"in Christ" is compared with our friendships.

There is a way forward here, devious and easily
overlooked, like a lane which is more easily seen when
one has already overshot it. It is by way of the idea of
partiality, which generally seems to be the chief obstacle
to taking friendship as a model for Christian love, but
which it is worth while now to look at in a different
light. A love which is partial, it seems, must be a selfish
love, not necessarily by being grasping but at any rate
in being biassed. Suppose though that instead of writing
it off as unredeemed or trying to deny its fundamentally
partial character, one accepts this character but takes
the moral disapproval out of it. The love here in question
is a love which *takes sides*, which loves someone in his
individuality and for his own special nature. It is probably
the most easily corruptible of all loves but that does
not make it essentially corrupt. The clearest example
is love of one's own self, and Christian moralists often
present this as a sum already worked out for us, to show
in one simple example how we are meant to love others.[2]

[1] cf. C. S. Lewis, *The Four Loves*, ch. IV. Teilhard de Chardin, *Human Energy*, p. 79.

[2] e.g., Wylie, *Human Nature and Christian Marriage*, p. 56, (S.C.M., 1958).

The next step in rescuing "partiality" is to point out that the lesson is made easier for us still. We do not have to jump straight from love of self to love of neighbour, for we have another example, not completely worked out but sketched in outline for us: the love of our friends, the people we find it easy to appreciate, the people to whom we are partial. In one's own case one can see what it is like for an individual to matter, in the case of the people one loves naturally one can see that this individual need not be oneself.[1] It should not be too hard to learn to extend this understanding ever more widely. Of course there is a danger in this so to speak teaching method that the pupil may get stuck in the examples and never move on beyond a selfish love of self, or only move on to a partial love of friends: that what is offered as a stepping stone could become a roost. But take the method at its best, and one can see in turn that "love of self" and "partiality" can be opened up, cleared of egoism and used to show in practice what appreciation means.

This may seem to have something to do with elementary Christian morality but not much to do with immanence, but only a little change of terminology is needed to bring out the relevance. What is partiality but *seeing from a point of view?* Initially, fundamentally and even tautologically one sees things from one's own point of view, but one is not limited to this. It is not a mere metaphor nor an unrealistic aspiration to say that one can enter into another person's point of view. To quote Brunner again,[2] "Love is not the recognition of the other person as an equal, but it is *identification* with the other person. Love not only recognises the claim of the other, but makes that claim *her own*." To have approached this rather "immanentist" concept of identification by means of the idea of partiality is to be less likely than usual to set up a kind of immune reaction to it, for one is in a position to see just how specific and concrete a concept it can be.

[1] cf. Ruth Saw, "The logic of the particular case", *Proceedings of the Aristotelian Society* (1965-6), pp. 10-11.

[2] *The Divine Imperative*, p. 326. (Italics mine.)

To be specific and concrete might not be so urgent if one were talking only about relationships between human beings, for any vagueness and abstractness would swiftly be shown up by the actual relationships in their everyday reality. But the time has come now to be brave enough to try to make some definite application of what has been said so far to the much more elusive relationship between people and God which has been kept in the background all along. If human immanence is to be used to illuminate divine, there comes a moment when the positive attempt must be made, and at this juncture the notion which has come to the surface again or, not to mix the metaphor, reappeared out of the darkness, is the notion of identification with a point of view.

The suggestion was made at a much earlier stage[1] that if a person is "a kind of living point of view" one might be able to make some sense of the idea of an infinite God as an infinite point of view, or rather as a being for whom all points of view are "assembled".[2] The intended upshot of the ensuing discussion has been as it were to fill in morally this key concept of a point of view, so that instead of seeming to be a merely abstract collecting centre for experiences it can stand for what one means by a *person* in a fully human sense: a being that matters, a centre of concerns, integrally related to other such beings. If all this has been proper, to come back now to affirm that God sees from all points of view is to affirm something that means a good deal, not just as an intellectual truth but as something for the religious imagination to grasp.

One can seem to begin to apprehend

> what God is, what we are
> What life is – how God tastes an infinite joy
> In infinite ways – one everlasting bliss,
> From whom all being emanates, all power
> Proceeds; in whom is life for evermore,
> Yet whom existence in its lowest form

[1] pp. 33-4.
[2] See above, p. 34. cf. Austin Farrer, *Faith and Speculation*, p. 154, (A. & C. Black, 1967).

Includes; where dwells enjoyment there is he:
With still a flying point of bliss remote,
A happiness in store afar, a sphere
Of distant glory in full view; thus climbs
Pleasure its heights for ever and for ever.[1]

The suggestion is that God's presence everywhere
in the world involves much more than academic awareness, that "concern" in its, so to speak, thickest sense
applies to God as well as to human persons, except
that the diversity of His concern is infinite. God loves
each creature: but even "each" is still too abstract
here, and to bring out the full sense one must risk the
subjective, "God loves *me*": not externally but with a
"partial" love which enters completely and as of right
into my unique point of view. "Before him no creature
is hidden, but all are open and laid bare to the eyes of
him with whom we have to do."[2] It is not obscure,
though it may be terrifying, to claim that God abides
in me in this sense, that He associates Himself to the
point of identification with the pettiness as well as the
glory of every creature He has made.[3]

Of course this emphasis is morally perilous and it is
not the sort of peril which ought to be ignored on the
ground that what is dangerous can none the less be
true, when what the danger consists in is the establishment
of a false picture. The claims of human value and indeed
of one's own value seem to be set misleadingly high:
how dare one think of divine partiality in this way?
But the misleading image itself yields place to a more
adequate way of thinking. "Out of this nettle, danger,
we pluck this flower, safety." The possibly spurious
comfort of being utterly appreciated is more than
balanced by the corresponding necessity of acknowledging that it is by infinite love that one is appreciated
utterly. To form the idea that God is the "ground of
one's being" in the sense that He is more concerned

[1] Browning, *Paracelsus* (last act).
[2] Hebrews 4: 13, See also above, p. 106.
[3] cf. Norman H. Snaith, *The Distinctive Ideas of the Old Testament*, p. 135, (Epworth Press, 1944). C. S. Lewis, *Undeceptions*, p. 121, (Bles, 1971).

for one, more "partial" to one, more on one's side,
than one is oneself; that one's humanly private point of
view is so to say anchored on to the divine: is assuredly
to feel that one has "got more than one bargained for".
One had indeed thought that one mattered and lived,
perhaps strenuously, upon that assumption. The affection
of one's family and friends had borne out this conviction
agreeably, and so to say manageably. But really to
matter, to matter to infinity as the individual creature
one is, is an idea so overwhelming as, curiously enough,
to put one's own puny pretensions in their place. In
such an interpretation of divine immanence in one's
own self an authentic Christian humility might take
root. The very limitations of this understanding could
be as it were self-correcting. The uniqueness it claims
for oneself is by its very nature manifold. One could
not begin to "take to heart" the presence of God in
this sense without having one's imagination stretched,
pulled out as it were into more of His concerns. To
"abide in Him", to enter into His love, could be a
practical corollary of His abiding in me, not just a
symmetrical literary flourish.

It is plain that by now one has begun to say things
about relationship with God which are only remotely
analogical to things one can say about relationships
between people; but this is quite as it should be. The
purpose of continuing with an analogical approach so
pertinaciously was to keep in touch with reality rather
than to propound dogmatically but obscurely what
relationship to God must be like. But analogy could
never be the last word. If in happy anthropomorphism
one pursues it too whole-heartedly one will fall into the
trap of proving too much which is a besetting danger
of this kind of theology.[1] The more one is inspired by the
belief that man is made in God's image and that there
are therefore analogies for the seeking, the less one dare
shut one's eyes to the awkward fact that what obliged
one to start the enquiry at all was the evident difference

[1] See above, p. 182.

between God and man. In the end this difference is bound to catch up with one. As Saint Augustine was constrained to end his great search for analogies for the Trinity "not with argument but with prayer",[1] so those who are still pursuing theological enquiries must not have the presumption to be drawn by their own arguments into losing touch with their terms of reference.

Again the error could be self-correcting. If the argument is allowed to swing naturally between analogy and contrast they can be presented as complementing not destroying one another. It began with contrast: that the standard case of relationship between two people just is face-to-face encounter; that Christianity in calling God personal certainly claims something for which such face-to-face encounter would be the obvious analogue; but that we cannot, by definition, meet face-to-face a being who has no body. The route which led around this obstacle leads on to fresh problems. First it was claimed, analogically, that in so far as people's bodies are *vehicles* of their presence it is not necessary to look on God as "bodiless", for it makes sense to say that He has many vehicles.[2] The Incarnational Deist was called in to explain that we have as much chance to "encounter" God or at least to identify Him as basic Christian personalism requires, for in Christ His presence in the physical world is writ large. Where the Incarnational Deist comes to the end of his resources is where Christianity starts to reach beyond face-to-face encounter and to insist that God is more than "a" person.

This was the point at which the argument took on a somewhat distinctive character, for in leaving the Incarnational Deist behind it declined to leave anthropomorphism behind with him, but rather renewed the search for analogies. Instead of saying in reverent defeatism "But God is different", it looked further at human relationships, among which after all the "face-to-face" pattern is only one among many. The suggestion is that the more complex ways in which people are capable of impinging upon one another do indeed provide ways of

---

[1] *De Trinitate* XV: 50.
[2] See above, p. 35.

approach to the supernatural "unity-in-plurality" that Christianity finds itself affirming.

But the more useful this approach proves, the less need there is to be totally carried away by it. What one may hope is to arrive at a position where, just because analogy has brought one so far, suddenly contrast becomes illuminating rather than baffling. If one follows analogy hopefully to the point where the path stops, there is a good chance of finding not a chasm across one's way but a glimpse of the panorama one has come to look at. One can lift up one's eyes and see that God is utterly different from other human beings and that one's relationship with Him must be unique: but at the same time not discontinuous with the familiar relationships one has been exploring.

Having turned a deaf ear all this while to those who have been reverently insisting that human relationships and divine are incommensurable, at last one can start to do their warnings justice. The argument has gone something like this: We are people, God is a person. But, God is much more than "a" person. But then, so are we, if that means separate shut-in units. It is when this has been appreciated that one can add with open eyes another "But", not repudiating the analogy but rounding it off with a contrast: that still, compared with God, finite creatures are in a way shut in upon themselves. Physical bodies are vehicles, but they are also fortresses: God, who can use any vehicle, is not liable to be imprisoned in any fortress. He can come and go as He will. "Scripture", says Otto,[1] "knows no 'Omnipresence' . . . it knows only the God who is where He wills to be, and is not where He wills not to be, the *deus mobilis*, who is no mere universally extended being, but an august mystery, that comes and goes, approaches and withdraws, has its time and its hour, and may be far or near in infinite degrees, 'closer than breathing' to us or miles remote from us." Or, as Augustine put it more succinctly, "The closed heart does not bar thy sight into it, nor does the hardness of our heart hold back thy hands."[2]

[1] *The Idea of the Holy*, Appendix VIII, p. 214.
[2] *Confessions* V: 1.

So at last one can gratefully say goodbye or perhaps *au revoir* to the human analogies without being obliged at the same time to say goodbye to intelligibility. In so far as the argument has carried conviction it has led towards a concept of relationship to God satisfyingly, not despairingly, different from relationships with other people. God's mystery belongs to His infinity, not to perverse mystification. "Immanence" is not a high-sounding piece of gratuitous nonsense but something human beings characteristically tend towards in various entirely specific ways but cannot fully achieve. It has to do with unity of concern amounting to a sort of identification though not to identity; or, to put it less prosaically but just as accurately, with love understood as a dimension of reality. This moral "thickening", so to say, must be put in if the world we live in is to be fully described.[1] If one can comprehend this humanly one has gained the right to try to put into words what it could amount to for the immanence of God. One can try to hold together the two pictures of a concern more relentlessly single-minded for each individual than the most complete egoist has for himself, yet more manifold than the stars in the sky: wholly honest, wholly undeceived, with the warmth of emotion without its weakness. In this way it becomes possible to give some "filling" to the intellectual belief that God abides in us for those who cannot claim to understand it by overwhelming personal experience and are not willing to fall back upon cliché or pretence.

What warrant is there for saying any of this at all? The only warrant is that it seems to follow, step by step, from what people have been led to say about God and human beings when they have taken the claims of the Christian Gospel as worth consideration. In other words, the Incarnational Deist has now handed over to a more adventurous friend of his, a sort of Incarnational Pantheist, whose credentials are somewhat similar. The argument likewise starts with certain traditions about a God, and a certain historical man, Jesus of Nazareth. He connects these in such a fashion as to create problems about the unity-in-plurality of persons,

[1] *See above*, p. 144.

and he offers a way of trying to handle these problems which suggests that certain sorts of relationships could be there to be entered into. Nothing has been proved. The attempt has been made to put the case in a definite enough form that at least it ought to be apparent what the argument is about, that one could tell what there is to believe or disbelieve. The test must be whether in this world or the next people do indeed find themselves able to enter these relationships.

CHAPTER THIRTEEN

Trinitarian Pantheism

The object of all this discussion has not been to build
a complete edifice but to construct a framework steady
enough to support the structure of Christian doctrine
as the skilled artisans require. It remains to consolidate
a little and to indicate some directions in which work
on the site could proceed.

First of all care is needed to make it plain that
"immanence" is not being set up as a rival to "transcendence" but that it is possible and convincing to present
the concepts in thoroughly traditional fashion as complementary aspects of Deity.[1] God can enter into His
creatures not because they are after all the whole of
His being but on the contrary because they are not.
It is as a being in His own right that He impinges upon
them. Although one wants to say that this "impinging"
is much more fundamental than just pushing them about,
that its relationship between Creator and creature is
somehow intrinsic, not external like that of a potter and
his pot, one also wants to say that it is quite different
from pantheistic absorption. It faces, so to speak, the
other way: it is more like a holding apart within a
basic unity than a running together or merging. God
upholds, God participates in, God is even identified
with, every creaturely point of view, but He does not
swallow up His creatures' existence nor do they constitute
the whole of His. One finds oneself able to make statements
like this about God because one is already making statements not dissimilar only much more limited about

[1] cf. C. H. Dodd, *The Epistle of Paul to the Romans*, pp. 136–7.
David Jenkins, *The Glory of Man*, p. 104.
O. Quick, *The Christian Sacraments*, p. 45, (Nisbet, 1932 edition).
Helen Oppenheimer, *The Character of Christian Morality*, p. 45.
cf. above, p. 182.

human relationships, because in fact one is able to balance analogy and contrast. "We are not", insists Bishop John Robinson,[1] "like rays to the sun or leaves to the tree": rather, we enjoy a personal freedom grounded in love.

"Panentheism" the name favoured by Dr. Robinson for this sort of understanding[2] is an ugly word with the limited and limiting character of a technical term; it touches off no exciting sparks and releases no inspiring images; but it must be admitted to have a certain convenient accuracy as a summary of a Christian account of divine immanence. What it means should be a Christian commonplace, that God is in the world but is not exhausted by it, that immanence allows for transcendence. This is admittedly not a strong enough instrument to serve as a real keyword opening up large fresh areas of thought. Its role is rather to be a useful label. Pedantic though it may seem, it could be worth while to make the effort, when one is trying to be analytical, to make use of this label to pick out the "unity-in-plurality" aspects of Christianity. Otherwise there is a risk that these aspects will either be ignored or be appropriated on behalf of that ancient skeleton-in-the-cupboard, pantheism. What "panentheism" does is single out better than "pantheism" the plurality in the unity. It is of course a skeleton itself in a different sense; it is no more than bare bones. The aim of the discussion since the first introduction of this technicality[3] has been the provision for this skeleton of some living flesh and blood. If unity-in-plurality can actually be located in human relationships it can come to seem much less arbitrary to apply the concept to relationships with God.

Why should "pantheism" have been such a name of terror, whose "siren song" changes to "the harpy rasp of moral horror"?[4] For the orthodox Christian any approach to identification or confusion of God with the world of nature is anathema for three reasons.

[1] *Honest to God*, p. 131.
[2] See above, p. 38.
[3] See above, ibid.
[4] Thomas McFarland, *Coleridge and the Pantheist Tradition*, p. 123, (Oxford, 1969).

First, it can lead straight to idolatry, making creatures into God, ignoring Augustine's powerful caution: "We are not God, but He made us".[1] Second, it risks committing the blasphemy of recognising God in the evil of the world as much as in the good. Third, it threatens to destroy the value of the individual, giving a human being "only a modal existence, as a wave momentarily cast up by the sea".[2]

The present approach has every right to claim to be less alarming, for it has precisely based itself upon the concept that the individual matters. It is as a subject of concern that one is capable of being indwelt by God. By seizing on to this idea one can establish a vantage point for the proper appreciation of God's presence in the whole of creation. Without either heresy or staleness one can dare to enter into Wordsworth's

> sense sublime
> Of something far more deeply interfused,
> Whose dwelling is the light of setting suns,
> And the round ocean and the living air,
> And the blue sky, and in the mind of man:
> A motion and a spirit, that impels
> All thinking things, all objects of all thought,
> And rolls through all things.[3]

One must still draw back though from calling oneself with him a "worshipper of Nature".[4]

Professor Zaehner refuses to class Wordsworth as a mystic since, he says surprisingly, "There is no trace of an actual experience at all, either of union with Nature or communion with God", only an "intimation" of "something which transcends and informs transient Nature".[5] For present purposes it is just such an intimation of transcendent immanence which is wanted, whether it is to be called "mysticism" or not. More severely, it was asserted by Aldous Huxley[6] that "A

---

[1] Confessions X: 6.
[2] MacFarland, ibid., p. 69.
[3] "Tintern Abbey".
[4] ibid.
[5] *Mysticism Sacred and Profane*, p. 35, (Oxford, 1957).
[6] Quoted N. Kemp Smith, "Is Divine Existence Credible?", printed in *Religion and Understanding*, ed. D. Z. Phillips, p. 115.

voyage through the tropics would have cured
[Wordsworth] of his too easy and confortable pantheism.
A few months in the jungle would have convinced him
that the diversity and utter strangeness of Nature are
at least as real and significant as its intellectually dis-
covered unity." Whether Wordsworth's own pantheistic
learnings were "easy and comfortable" or not, the sort
of pantheistic understanding of creation which is in
question at the moment is encouraged not damped by
this wilder emphasis. It is not a matter of all things
being one but of all things being indwelt by God's
presence.

Less well known than the Wordsworth lines, more
exotic, but not necessarily out of keeping with
Wordsworth's conviction, is the climax of Browning's
Paracelsus :[1]

> The centre-fire heaves underneath the earth,
> And the earth changes like a human face;
> The molten ore bursts up among the rocks,
> Winds into the stone's heart . . . .
> God joys therein. The wroth sea's waves are edged
> With foam, white as the bitten lip of hate,
> When, in the solitary waste, strange groups
> Of young volcanos come up, cyclops-like,
> Staring together with their eyes on flame –
> God tastes a pleasure in their uncouth pride . . . .
> . . . . . Savage creatures seek
> Their loves in wood and plain – and God renews
> His ancient rapture. There he dwells in all,
> From life's minute beginnings, up at last
> To man – the consummation of His scheme
> Of being, the completion of this sphere
> Of life.

Admirers of Teilhard de Chardin will surely not find
this an unfamiliar vision. Gerard Manley Hopkins
summarised something not unlike it: "The world is
charged with the grandeur of God."
Without idolatry one can think in terms of worshipping

---
[1] Going on from the lines quoted above, pp. 190–1.

God not exactly in but through Nature, especially in the zestful abundance of wholly non-utilitarian delights, like the Psalmist's "Leviathan whom you made to amuse you".[1] One has one's own catalogue of theophanies. A meadow full of springy tough light-coloured flowers, a school of brilliant purple fish seen in an aquarium, the tapestry reds and greens of a field of tomatoes, a piece of wild thyme caught in the door of a car, can be means of grace, "hints and hopes",[2] not proofs but as it were carriers of the glory of God. "One's mind runs back up the sunbeam to the sun."[3] Perhaps even evils can be, when he chooses, God's vehicles;[4] though not in Christian thinking His features. He can come to meet us in them.[5] One could learn to find God everywhere without plunging "into that abyss of mysticism in which God himself is nothing".[6] But the condition of all this is that God is more than His manifestations. He takes part in their existence, like Keats and the sparrow,[7] but He does not lose Himself in them.

The historical safeguard of the transcendence of God against any heretical pantheism has been the doctrine of the Trinity. It is a doctrine which really comes to life for those religious thinkers who feel the pull of both immanence and transcendence. According to C. C. J. Webb[8] "It has been said that no one can really claim to be a philosopher who has not undergone a 'bath of Spinoza': that is, who has not at any rate felt something of that intellectual passion for unity which drove Spinoza into his doctrine of a single Substance. . . . A man may have passed through his 'bath of Spinoza' and ended in a position in which he can affirm personality in God and freedom in man in a sense in which Spinoza would deny them; but his affirmation is not what it would have been, had he never seriously felt at all the sting of

---

[1] Psalm 104: 26, Jerusalem Bible.
[2] See above, p. 52.
[3] C. S. Lewis, *Letters to Malcolm*, p. 118, (Bles, 1964).
[4] See above, pp. 37–8.
[5] cf. J. A. T. Robinson, *Exploration into God*, p. 109f.
[6] R. G. Collingwood, *Speculum Mentis*, p. 127, (Oxford, 1924).
[7] Letter to Benjamin Bailey, Saturday, 22nd November, 1817.
[8] *Pascal's Philosophy of Religion*, p. 26.

the thought which inspires what is commonly, in speaking
of Spinoza, called his *pantheism*.''[1] For many a Christian
thinker and not least for C. C. J. Webb himself,[2] it has
been the Trinitarian structure of Christian doctrine
which has enabled him to keep his head above the water.
A recent account[3] of the thought of Coleridge is of more
than just literary or biographical interest here. Fascinated
and yet repelled by the doctrine of Spinoza, and unable
in his intellectual integrity to discount it, he came
gradually to the point of confessing that "Pantheism is
but a painted Atheism and that the Doctrine of the
Trinity is the great and only sure Bulwark against it".[4]
This is not just polemics. It shows Coleridge struggling
to keep in focus the concept of a personal God,[5] neither
too distinct from the world to enter into it nor too
dependent upon the world to transcend it. To trace out
the various influences upon him and their ramifications
in his developing thought is to feel the "sting" of
pantheism oneself and to begin to appreciate the need
for the "Trinitarian solution" that "guaranteed the
existence of both the Many and the One, and so allowed
him to anchor his complete system . . . in an extra-
mundane ground without abandoning the reality of the
natural world".[6] In other words, it does not seem unreasonable to say that it is Trinitarian doctrine, with its
affirmation that the Deity has a transcendent complete-
ness of personal life, that best allows one to use the
terminology of "vehicles" rather than of absorption
when one needs also to talk about His immanence.

The doctrine of the Trinity affirms that the God with
whom Christians are supposed to enter into personal
relationship is not simply one Person but is somehow
three. Relationship within God comes before any relationship between God and the world and it is in this eternal

[1] cf. Farrer, *The Glass of Vision*, pp. 7–8, quoted above pp. 51–2.
[2] *Problems in the Relations of God and Man*, e.g., pp. 231, 249, quoted above,
p. 116. See also ibid., pp. 234–5. See also much of *God and Personality* and
Divine Personality and Human Life.
[3] Thomas McFarland, *Coleridge and the Pantheist Tradition*.
[4] *Philosophical Lectures*, p. 271, quoted McFarland, p. 198.
[5] McFarland, p. 236.
[6] ibid., p. 227.

unity-in-plurality that Christians hope somehow to take part. What urgently needs to be kept clear at any stage in the argument where this doctrine emerges into explicitness is how far it is problem and how far it is answer.[1]

What it is not is an *explanation* of divine immanence. On the contrary, if it had been made more prominent any earlier in the argument it could only have aggravated the difficulties. It has been in the background all this time[2] as something a full doctrine of immanence would have to explain. But now that one has made a certain amount of progress an appeal to the doctrine of the Trinity can serve in two ways to establish more securely the view which has been sketched. First, it has just been suggested that a firm hold on the fact that Christianity is trinitarian can be and has historically been a *safeguard* against any account of immanence that runs away with itself into heretically pantheistic absorption of the individual. But secondly, one has now arrived at a point at which the doctrine of the Trinity can constructively be used as a *test case*. If the understanding of unity-in-plurality which one has been approaching can even make the difficult dogma of three Persons in one God seem a little less obscure, one can be encouraged to think that one is indeed on the right lines. The hope is that instead of stumbling from common sense to contradiction one can catch a glimpse of what Professor Schillebeeckx has called a "reciprocal illumination",[3] a promise of a two-way traffic between the divine and the human.

There seems to be an opening up of possibilities, a lifting of the mist in this doctrinal territory, in two directions. First, the stark paradox of the dogma of three Persons in one God is eased when human persons are themselves not seen as sharply separated units but as fundamentally bound to one another.[4] Secondly,

---

[1] cf. I. T. Ramsay, "A Personal God", *Prospect for Theology*, ed. F. G. Healey, p. 56, (Nisbet, 1966).

[2] See above, pp. 112–3.

[3] E. Schillebeeckx, *Marriage: Secular Reality and Saving Mystery*, Vol. 1, p. 63, (Sheed & Ward, translation, 1965).

[4] See R. C. Moberly, *Atonement and Personality*, p. 157, (John Murray, 1901).

there is a hope of coming to a better appreciation at last of the Christian doctrine of the Holy Spirit.

It is not just a debating point to say that the doctrine of the Trinity in relation to Jewish monotheism is like the complications of Einstein in relation to Newtonian physics. The comparison of theological with scientific paradox has often been made too glibly, but it is none the less a fair one here, for in each case one sees a tradition which enjoyed a beautiful and compact analysis of its subject-matter thrown into disorder, but constructive disorder, by the necessity to hold firmly to two sets of given but recalcitrant data.

To put it very roughly, one might say that the need for a complicated monotheism arose because it seemed proper to worship Christ who himself worshipped the Father. So the doctrine is fairly claimed to have an empirical foundation, a basis in experience. But going on from this beginning the doctrine, for all its difficulty, has proved profoundly satisfying morally and meta-physically: not least to those for whom the One and the Many is a real problem, for whom a God who was sheerly One would be either out of relation with the world or entirely lost in it.

Still it remains acutely paradoxical and the pressure is inevitably strong either to let the scales drop heavily on one side or to give up the whole thing in despair. It must be apparent that the personalist emphasis with which the present argument began leans strongly towards what has been called the "social" theory of the Trinity, preferring the risk of tritheism to any kind of Sabellian doctrine which would leave God in "unattended, unresponsive solitude".[1] It falls in very contentedly with Dr. Hodgson's argument of thirty years ago[2] for doing justice to the plurality, to the relationships, in God even if that should mean leaving the unity as an unfathomable mystery.[3] But there is no need to become narrowly partisan about the "social theory", shutting one's eyes to the equally impressive arguments on the other side,

[1] Prestige, *Fathers and Heretics*, p. 79, (S.P.C.K., 1954).
[2] *The Doctrine of the Trinity*, Croall lectures, 1942–3, (Nisbet, 1943).
[3] ibid., e.g., 108, 141, 175.

if only one is in a position to allow that even human relationships are less cut-and-dried than one might suppose. Three *or* One is not a question which has to be raised with such sharpness as to drive people into heresy.

What matters, from the present point of view, is that "the divine Life is itself not bare unity but community".[1] In affirming this the temptation of the personalist is to stress the Trinity at the expense of the Unity, and in just such a way heresy is classically formed, in the whole-hearted appreciation of one side of a truth. Instead one must remind oneself that "God is not a committee";[2] that the term "Person" as historically used in trinitarian theology did not have its modern meaning; and that for many Christians it is God's oneness, not His plurality, which must be seized and held at whatever cost.

Honesty seems to force one to keep on asking, Is God one centre of consciousness or three? Personalism craves for the answer, three; but a vast weight of authority insists that this is tritheism.[3] It is at this juncture that one finds oneself taking refuge in vagueness or paradox in the name of orthodoxy; but suddenly, it is at this juncture that one can begin to reap some benefit from the route by which one has come. For what is needed here as a safeguard from tritheism is a concept which has been approached again and again at different levels in this whole discussion, never quite reached but constantly looked at, familiar enough by now to have established a certain solidarity which is not entirely spurious: the concept of indwelling, of personal immanence, of unity-in-plurality. It is at its least paradoxical when it is given a moral "filling" by way of the notion of "concern". If this concept of "a union which does not destroy but fulfils the distinctive character of its constituent elements"[4] is already available, applicable

[1] Burnaby, *Amor Dei*, p. 306.
[2] Baker, *The Foolishness of God*, p. 312.
[3] e.g., Welch, *The Trinity in Contemporary Theology* (S.C.M., 1953), musters the arguments strongly.
[4] A. M. Allchin in a review of a book on F. D. Maurice, *Theology* (October 1965), p. 489. This phrase has for long summed up for me the concept I have been pursuing.

in various partial ways to human life, then the mystery of the Trinity can be approached as continuous with the depths of human existence, not as a perverse departure from common-sense understanding.

It is only fair to admit that this whole approach, not only the "social theory" but the attempt to illuminate Trinitarian theory by a more flexible approach to the notion of personality as such, has been weightily repudiated by the American scholar Dr. Claude Welch. He denies that the interdependence of persons proves that personality is essentially "permeable";[1] he enquires how such "permeability" could stop short of complete merging;[2] and he concludes that if one begins with a social analogy for the Trinity one can get no further than tritheism.[3] He even brings in, to dismiss, the contemporary *sociological* picture of mankind as essentially social and personality as " 'open' rather than a closed, discrete, independent entity":[4] his preference is evidently for stressing the distinctness of individuals.[5] Three things may be said in reply. First, it is the whole line of the present argument, not just a paragraph in place here, which must stand to confront Dr. Welch's attack. Secondly, if one feels more acutely than he does the personalist pressure to deny the solitariness of the Deity, one will be more ready to receive the "social" arguments. Thirdly, the present discussion has not been intended precisely as a defence of any particular theory of the Trinity, but as a suggestion that if one takes "unity of concern" as an available keyword the statements which theologians have found themselves making do in practice seem less obscure.

For example, when one comes from this direction the technical term *perichoresis*, or mutual interpenetration of the three Persons,[6] instead of cropping up as a baffling complication, can seem to fill a gap in one's comprehen-

---

[1] *The Trinity in Contemporary Theology* (first published 1952), p. 258.
[2] ibid., p. 257.
[3] ibid., p. 259.
[4] ibid., p. 258.
[5] ibid., p. 259.
[6] See Prestige, *God in Patristic Thought*, pp. xxxii–xxxiii and ch. XIV (S.P.C.K., 1952 edition).

sion. One can appreciate better the enthusiasm with which theologians tend to arrive at it.[1] With the idea of the "receptiveness" to each other of the Persons,[2] it promises to call up personal and not only spatial images in one's mind. Is one merely imposing modern prejudices upon ancient technicality? The hope is rather that one might release the ancient technicality into modern usefulness, and so enter into a continuing tradition. Certainly originality here would be wholly out of place.

This hope of illumination is maintained when one comes to consider how the Holy Spirit fits into the picture.[3] One has tended to start with two irreconcilable models. On the one hand there is the separate being in whom one is committed to believe as the Third Person of the Trinity, characteristically pictured as the dove descending from on high at a particular moment or whispering confidentially into the ear of a saint.[4] On the other hand there is the diffused reality of the Spirit as an aspect of the relationship between other persons: the love by which the Father loves the Son, the Inner Light within us, a sort of area or realm into which one can enter rather than a person one can meet. With all this floating somewhat unintegrated in their minds, Christians worry about not finding the Holy Ghost as real as the Father or the Son, and reproach themselves and the Church for neglecting Him. There is an answer here which is excellent as far as it goes: that as the Spirit is the light by which we see other things, we could not expect to look directly at Him.[5] One drives by car at night, helped by one's own headlamps, dazzled by everyone else's. Just so, God's transcendence dazzles, His immanence illuminates but cannot be looked at, The Spirit is God immanent: yes indeed; but then, *why do we call the Spirit He?* The trouble with the "light"

---

[1] e.g., Welch, *The Trinity in Contemporary Theology*, p. 116. D. M. Baillie, *God was in Christ*, p. 141.

[2] Prestige, *God in Patristic Thought*, pp. 33, 289.

[3] See above, p. 110.

[4] e.g., at the Benedictine monastry at Subiaco about fifty miles east of Rome.

[5] e.g., C. S. Lewis, *The Four Loves*, p. 143. Psalm 36 : 9.

model is not that it is inadequate,[1] for any model must eventually be that, but that it is wholly irrelevant to what many people feel to be the main difficulty. It elucidates immanence in terms of what is impersonal instead of facing the problem of how it can possibly make sense to speak of a *Person* as immanent. It is only by a line of argument which tends to break down the apparently irreducible separateness of individual persons that one can come to have an inkling of what it could mean to talk of an indwelling personal Spirit, and so to see this aspect of the doctrine of the Trinity as something to do with reality.

By taking this route through areas of analogy and contrast into the idea of divine immanence as characteristically personal, one can now begin to approach nearer to the biblical and traditional understanding of the presence of God within the human soul.[2] At an earlier stage[3] one could only put one's faith rather helplessly in the thought that He must be there, for lack of any sign of face-to-face confrontation. One has the right now to begin to enter into that region of one's Christian heritage to be found in texts such as "When we cry, 'Abba! Father!' it is the Spirit himself bearing witness with our spirit that we are children of God".[4] The ancient formula for Christian prayer, more honoured than comprehended, that it should be "to the Father, through the Son, in the Spirit"[5] can come to life as something to be attempted, not only in public but in private prayer, not only by mature Christians but as a lesson for learners. Even Saint Augustine's "that you may love God, let Him dwell in you and love Himself through you"[6] seems to signify something possible. It is a more positive and grander way of expressing the idea of that divine

[1] See above, p. 45.
[2] Magnificently expounded by Dr. Farrer, for instance in "The Hidden Spring", a sermon on the theme "with thee is the well of life, and in thy light we shall see light", printed in *A Celebration of Faith*, (Hodder and Stoughton, 1970).
[3] See above, pp. 68, 87.
[4] Romans 8: 14–16. See above, p. 111.
   See also, Romans 8: 26; Galatians 4: 6.
[5] See above, p. 91.
[6] Quoted in Burnaby, *Amor Dei*, p. 176.

partiality which takes the individual up into the love of God, not by disregarding his particular point of view but by entering into it with infinite thoroughness. Once one has got rid of the barrier to understanding set up by the supposition that persons, human or divine, must be distinct self-contained pellets if they are to be real existents at all, one can come to see such expressions as "the causal root of our being"[1] as potentially an answer to one's questions rather than as merely perplexing. This position could hardly have been arrived at, once the difficulties had begun to be felt, by simply affirming "But God is quite different" at the outset.

[1] Austin Farrer, *Faith and Speculation*, p. 47.

CHAPTER FOURTEEN

Indwelling and Incarnation

If any progress in the comprehension of immanence has been made at all it is important not to lose it by eventually letting all the problems run together into one indistinct mass. It could be easier than ever to fall into a comfortable theological jargon, to let unclarified assumptions spread themselves over real situations so as to blur every outline. The presence of a human being is not one simple idea: still less the presence of God. Unless the different kinds of things one wants to say about His presence are kept reasonably distinct at last nothing will have been gained. One will find oneself making claims in such vague and diffuse or in such overweening terms that sincere and specific faith becomes almost impossible.

The remedy is to be definite even at the cost of being extremely elementary. The foundation of a Christian doctrine of immanence is the belief in God the Creator, who is able at His own will to be present in His creatures and use them as "vehicles", to take cognisance of the physical world and impinge upon it from any point of view. How such Christian belief is arrived at and justified by apologetics is not the present question.[1] How it can be given a definite enough content to make it worth discussing has been the main theme of this book. In this context the doctrine of the Trinity has a convincing cogency, for it places the concept of immanence within God's own life in such a fashion as to safeguard also His transcendence when one comes to speak of Him in relation to the world. There seems to be the possibility of a two-way illumination between the unity-in-plurality a Christian affirms within the being of God, and the

[1] But see above, ch. IV.

unity-in-plurality which is an image of this in His relationships with His creatures. To put it naively, if God has a
life of His own He can enter into relationships with His
creatures while maintaining His distinctness from them.
The discussion could go on in various ways here.
It could continue to explore the being of God Himself,
seeking to understand better what kind of thing one is
trying to say when one makes affirmations about the
Trinity in Unity. It could talk about the awareness of
God in nature, probably making use of the distinction
between pantheism and panentheism. It could discuss
in Old Testament terms the activity of God in history
and how He can use even wicked men as His vehicles.
It could expatiate upon the particular self-identification
of God with the oppressed and downtrodden and the
need to recognise Him in our fellow-men. More theologically still and no less morally, it could aspire to the high
doctrine that the bond of unity between ourselves and
God is the very same as the bond of unity within God
Himself:[1] that creatures are actually to enter into the
life of the Trinity.

These are all possible lines for the Trinitarian Pantheist
to take, and they all require, and deserve, exploration;
but they all have one thing in common, that not one
of them takes heed of the position of the Incarnational
Deist, left behind a long way back in the argument but
never entirely repudiated. The function of the Incarnational Deist was as it were to mediate between the
theologian and the apologist. If the theologian claims
to say what belief in God means, the Incarnational
Deist will not let him leave such talk in the air, unattached
to reality. He will try to find out to what facts it is suitable
to apply it, if it is supposed to have any real significance.
He can then hand over to the apologist the task of showing
that the facts do indeed give rise to the theology.

The Incarnational Deist's understanding was that the
presence of God is focused in Christ. The Trinitarian
Pantheist has been able more ambitiously but less
precisely to talk about God's presence with Himself as

[1] cf. Thornton, *The Common Life in the Body of Christ*, p. 294, (Dacre Press,
1950 edition).

expanding or overflowing to become His presence in the world. But if these two styles of understanding are both to be attempted they will have to be related to each other. If God's presence is distinctively to be found in the life of Christ, some effort must be made to distinguish His immanence in Christ from His immanence in creatures as soon as one wants to say that He is not immanent *only* in Christ; or the whole concept of God's presence to which one has tried to give some precision will be lost again in vagueness.

The justification for Incarnational Deism was that it was truly incarnational. It could cope with the difficulty of recognising God's presence in the world with any confidence, because it claimed to identify God's presence in Christ. God may be a bodiless Being, but He has His own specific point of view in the physical world from which He can act and in which He can be recognised. Having affirmed this the Incarnational Deist can then gracefully move aside, not ignominiously retreat, to make room for those who make wider claims for God's presence. He can even come to allow in Athanasius' famous phrase that the Word "was made man that we might be made God",[1] that what Christ is we can be. But he will spoil his case if in aspiring towards the deification of man he loses touch with his original conviction of the uniqueness of Christ. This claim was definite enough to affirm: it could make up for the indefiniteness of other claims which become allowable in its light. It will be lost if one fails to insist as firmly as Athanasius himself that whatever human beings may become, the Son is God Himself incarnate, not a creature on the same sort of footing as others who happen to have taken on a special role. If one is going to combine successfully the honesty of the Incarnational Deist's starting point with the greater richness of the Trinitarian Pantheist's talk about immanence, one must go on insisting upon God's presence in Christ in a more fundamental sense than in other human beings. Christ, that is, is archetype not merely example.

If Incarnation is to be distinguished from other kinds

[1] *De Incarnatione,* 54.

of indwelling and not just assimilated to them it is important not to let the argument freewheel. "Unity of concern" has been emphasised: what could seem more natural and promising than to expound the theme of the total unity of concern of Jesus of Nazareth with God? If the mystery of the Trinity has been illuminated along these lines, why not this other "mystery of coinherence", the unity of the divine and the human in Christ? It is fair in resisting this pressure to point out that one is unlikely to underestimate the uniqueness of the concept of the Trinity, so that analogies there are less dangerous; whereas it is a standing temptation to reduce the idea of the presence of God in Christ to not more than a particular instance of divine grace. It would be elegant and comprehensive if one could expound both these great mysteries in corresponding ways, but such tidiness is not inevitably correct. Just so at an earlier stage in the argument, when among human relationships the unity-in-plurality of marriage was being used as an illustration of immanence, it could have been tempting simply to slip in parenthood as if it were a parallel example,[1] so blurring distinctions rather than clarifying them.

Parenthood would have been an unhelpful example of immanence because in the western world it is not, at its best, an illustration of unity. The Incarnation on the other hand does not typically exemplify immanence in the sense developed here because the kind of unity involved requires to be too distinctive. The "unity of concern" terminology is a way of comparing relationships rather than of contrasting them. To try to account for the doctrine of the Incarnation adequately in terms of the *unity of concern* of a particular man with God could be to stretch the concept so far that it loses, so to speak, its elasticity, becoming ineffective elsewhere where it could have been useful.

Once the special character of the Incarnation has been posited, then the comparisons can be constructively explored. There is no need, for example, to set permanently aside D. M. Baillie's insight that Christ is the supreme example of "the paradox of grace",[1] nor H. R. Macintosh's illuminating phrase, "absolute immanence."[2] It could be enlightening, along these lines, to speak for instance of the transparency of people to one another and to God. Where the rest of us are in various degrees opaque, Christ was absolutely transparent to God and so capable of receiving and transmitting His grace. To say this sort of thing is not false or unimportant but could be premature, when what is being sought is a way of expounding the doctrine that *the Word was made flesh*, that God actually entered into human life. The ancient concept of pre-existence still requires emphasis.

Such an insistence is old-fashioned today, ineradicably metaphysical as it is. If analogies drawn from human immanence only smother the differences between ourselves and Christ, how is God's presence in Christ to be talked about intelligibly without going back to the "Emperor's New Clothes" predicament? The hope must be that the doctrine of Incarnation, considered not just as one aspect of God's immanence but as owing its significance to its uniqueness, is sufficiently connected with reality and has enough impetus of its own to make headway itself, like a bicycle, without needing the immediate props of analogy. It affirms that Christ is even more than God's "vehicle": he is God embodied; and people have thought they have seen the point of this.

To take one's stand in this way upon Christ's pre-existence is not just an obstinate mythological speculation, but the necessary condition of the first Christian thinkers being right about his significance. Without some understanding that in becoming man he emptied himself, his sacrifice is reduced to an unhappy miscarriage of justice and the heavenly Father is left on high untouched by the evils of the world and unreconciled to man.[3] Any explanation that may eventually be given of how

---

[1] Developed in *God was in Christ*. See M. F. Wiles, "The Christology of D. M. Baillie", *Church Quarterly Review* (1963), especially pp. 63-4.

[2] *The Person of Jesus Christ*, cf. p. 434.

[3] cf. John Baker, *The Foolishness of God*, p. 308.

God can assume human life in this way will assuredly not be incongruous with what has been said about the meaning of personal immanence, but it will not take the short cut of making all kinds of indwelling seem alike. A most promising line of approach to the understanding of Incarnation as such has been suggested by the Rev. John Baker: "When God chooses to exist within the terms of our environment a man is what he becomes."[1] It is worth noticing in passing that to believe in Christ's pre-existent divinity does not involve the belief that he himself knew it on earth distinctly and completely. Dr. Farrer used to apply the philosophical distinction between "knowing how" to be God's Son and "knowing that" he was God's Son to the consciousness of Christ,[2] thereby at least easing the psychological difficulty even if leaving the metaphysical problem as difficult as ever, the problem of elucidating the eternal relationship "between the infinite divine 'I' and the 'someone' who was among men as Jesus."[3]

Suppose that the Incarnation has been set up as unique, this is no place for stopping. Take God's indwelling in Christ out of the problem of divine immanence and set it apart as being more fundamental: one will be confronted without respite by the problem of Christ's indwelling in us and ours in him.[4] Incarnational Deism, which concentrated on God in Christ, broke down, and it broke down not because what it said about Christ as a focus of God's presence proved unsatisfactory as far as it went, but because it could not say so much without being obliged to say a good deal more.[5] The mystery of Christ as it presented itself to the first Christians was more than the mystery of God's presence in this particular man: it was also the mystery of this man somehow turning out in their experience to be more than

---

[1] ibid., p. 311. See John Hick, "Christology at the Crossroads" in *Prospect for Theology*, ed. F. G. Healey.

[2] e.g., *Faith and Logic*, ed. Basil Mitchell, p. 103. *The Triple Victory*, pp. 59–60, (Faith Press, 1965).

[3] D. L. Edwards, *Journal of Theological Studies* (1971), p. 305, in a review of Mr. Baker's book.

[4] See above, pp. 19, 106–7.

[5] See above, pp. 105ff, 110–1.

a single individual.[1] This is no optional refinement of Christianity but part of its essential message; but it is an even stiffer test for a proposed account of immanence than the concept of divine immanence itself. The present argument has suggested that statements about immanence are not meaningless even when applied to human beings and can be allowed to have a fuller not a lesser meaning when applied to God. The movement of thought has been by way of analogy to contrast. But when it appears that there is a *man* who somehow belongs as much on the divine as on the human side of the comparison it cannot just be assumed that this further claim makes sense. It is imperative to go on to face two questions. The first is; How can divine immanence apply to a man? The second is, Does our Christian experience indeed yield a basis for such a claim?

It will be apparent that the first of these is in effect a re-posing of the problem about Incarnation that has just been hopefully evaded. If anything is clear from the sources it is that Jesus of Nazareth was an individual human being. It has been affirmed that the evidence suggests that this individual was God Incarnate, and that this statement is different in kind not only in degree from the statement that he was inspired, requiring in particular some kind of belief in his pre-existence. The suggestion was made that the problems, great as they are, of relating the person of Jesus to the Second Person of the Trinity can be put aside on the two grounds that the doctrine has an initial comprehensibility and that it is confusing to treat it as a problem of immanence. But now the difficulty comes rolling back like a mist, for it seems to be of the human Jesus Christ that it is said that we live in him and he in us. It is indubitably into his human nature, not even into his nature as God the Son, that we are characteristically said to be incorporated.[2] We are members of his Body, not just parts

---

[1] See above, p. 19. The matter was nicely put by Professor C. F. D. Moule in a short article, "The Resurrection", *The Franciscan* (Summer 1963).

[2] e.g., E. L. Mascall, *Via Media*, p. 148, (Longmans, 1956). See above, p. 109.

of a diffuse Spirit. Tillich was not really darkening New Testament counsel when he said that Christ is "absolutely concrete and absolutely universal".[1] Parts of the New Testament do appear to imply just that, whatever it can be thought to mean. Here is a seemingly historical man of whom statements are made which appear to be nonsense when applied to a finite being.

A final answer would be a full Christology. All that can be done here is to clear obstacles from the immediate path. These things are not being said just to make everything difficult, but because this was the experience which the early Christians had. It is evident from reading, for instance, St. Paul's epistles that this is not a man with a neat doctrinaire theory which all the facts must be forced to fit, but rather a man who has been driven out of just such a theory by a sort of explosion of fact for which he can hardly find coherent words. There is a pressure not his own making him say these paradoxical things: and his paradoxes are taken up and re-stated, not exactly but with satisfying variations, in the Johannine writings and the Synoptic Gospels themselves. Here at least one has some data which it is an authentic enterprise to try to interpret.

In this enterprise the concept of immanence has by no means exhausted its usefulness, so long as one keeps clear what can be done with it and what cannot. It can certainly be used both for talking about God present in all His creatures and about His particular presence in Christ; but not then also to distinguish between these modes of presence and so account for Christ's uniqueness. Accept this limitation and there is still plenty to be said about the kinds of indwelling which Christians especially associate with Christ. There are continuities here not only discontinuities, and if the preceding argument has shown that immanence itself is not a wholly incomprehensible notion but has roots in human experience, there is scope for applying this line of thought to the kind of thing the New Testament says about human and Christian relationships.

[1] *Systematic Theology*, I, p. 20.

"Unity of concern" may not do justice to "The Word was made flesh", but it does potentially illuminate the Johannine concept of abiding in one another and in Christ: it characterises a bond which is both moral and objective, both ideal and real. Likewise "unity-in-plurality" may not do much to explain "God was in Christ", but it does fill out St. Paul's keyword "in Christ" as applied to Christians. It suggests that people can be united in ways which sheer individualism could not predict, and that to call them members of one another need be no mere metaphor.

These ways of speaking put one in a position to welcome the characteristically Christian insight that whatever union with God means, it is not something offered to isolated individuals. So one can pick up and strengthen the emphasis which the Incarnational Deist came to put upon Church and sacraments as an integral not a peripheral part of Christianity. Baptism to begin with is plainly incorporation into the Church. To say that this involves incorporation into Christ's Body is to go a step further, but a step which it is not too difficult to take when one has learnt the two lessons: to think of union without loss of identity, and to think of a body as essentially a vehicle for the presence of a person. Especially in a Eucharistic context, talk of being built up into one Body by partaking together of the bread and wine nominated by Christ to be his vehicles need not seem too obscurely metaphysical. As the bread and wine represent Christ, not remotely but objectively, so those who share them can be united with one another and can come themselves to represent him by becoming, in their unity, his bodily vehicle on earth. Hallowed words can inoculate one against meaning, but when one has tried to arrive at the meaning by a different route one can return to the hallowed words and find them expressing what one wants to say; in this case that people can become "very members incorporate in the mystical Body of Christ which is the blessed company of all faithful people."

Yet all this about how we can abide in Christ could be an evasion of what the New Testament says about

Christ himself: that since God came into humanity, or perhaps since the Ascension, or maybe better still *because* God came eternally into humanity, there is reciprocally *humanity in God*. This humanity is supposed to be as specific as Christ's physical body, as divine as the Risen Lord, as corporate as the Church, as available as the sacraments; and into it we are supposed to be incorporated. To say any of these things teases us out of thought, or should if we are prepared to concentrate. No amount of exploring the idea that finite immanence as we experience it can illuminate infinite immanence as we are taught to believe in it, can be much help in reckoning with the concept of a particular finite being to whom the sort of immanence which could only be characteristic of infinity is somehow ascribed. The question how such things can be said about a human person has an unanswered remainder which pushes one mercilessly into the second question about one's right to say them at all. Does being a Christian after all give one reason to talk like this?

The way one has come to this point is both dangerous and encouraging: dangerous, because having struggled so hard to maintain one's integrity and not make affirmations one cannot begin to understand, one might relax too soon, assuming that what one has said so far can automatically be re-applied; encouraging, because after all any clearing of the thicket which has been achieved suggests that it is not wholly impenetrable. The main thing is not to claim what one has *not* achieved, not for instance to say "we" where what one really means is "St. Paul and St. John and the people today who seem to know about these matters."[1] Honesty commends intellectually as much as morally Dame Julian of Norwich's saying that "thus is this medley so marvellous in us that scarcely we know of our self or of our even-Christian in what way we stand."[2] From such uncertainty rather than from complacency one can hope to advance.

When at last one comes to the point where Christian doctrine must either relate to Christian experience or

[1] cf. above, p. 130 note 4.
[2] *Revelations of Divine Love*, ch. LII.

fail to relate to it, one can take comfort in two ways. First, there is no need to belittle the extent to which the biblical writers were after all speaking in metaphors, and the amount of understanding which can come from exploring these quite straightforwardly without expecting paradox and metaphysics.[1] For instance, Professor Dodd, while not rejecting out of hand the "Christ-mysticism" which regards Christ "as a kind of spiritual space . . . within which the believer lives, as in an atmosphere," prefers, and surely constructively prefers, to understand the expression "in Christ" in the Pauline epistles in a more personal way. He goes back to the idea of "the solidarity of all believers in the body of Christ, which is the Church. "The metaphor," he explains, "is still spatial; but it is not a case of the individual living 'in Christ' as in a surrounding atmosphere, but of his forming part of an organic society in which Christ is active."[2] Such a concept of the divine humanity one can form in one's mind without metaphysical vertigo. Likewise there is scope for exploring the notions of Christ our representative, the Mediator, the *Head* of the Body. For their proper working out these ideas need his divinity and do not minimise his immanence; but they do not, so far, ask for a seeming individual to be also and essentially corporate.

Secondly, it is still worth saying in quite an obvious way that as a Christian I must start where I am and move on as I can. If I do not pretend that what is obscure is clear, I shall not be inhibited from trying to clarify it. There is hope that it can be clarified, a little from previous experience and much from the promise that "he that doeth the will shall know of the doctrine" taken not as a proof-text but as an element in the tradition. As the seventeenth-century Scottish divine William Guthrie said,[3] "They complain that they know not whether they be in Christ or not; but as few take pains to be in Him, so few take pains to try if they be in Him. It is

---

[1] Best, *One Body in Christ*, (S.P.C.K., 1955), is a good example of such exploration.

[2] *The Fourth Gospel*, p. 193, (Cambridge, 1953).

[3] Quoted by Geddes MacGregor in *Holiness*, ed. Marina Chavchavadze, p. 73, (Hodder and Stoughton, 1970).

a work and business which cannot be done sleeping." If incorporation into Christ is something I am actually promised, it follows that as I grow into it I shall be able to speak of it: provided I do not debase the whole idea by presuming upon it too soon. This proviso was the whole theme of the Incarnational Deist's message, and he will need to be recalled as often as it is forgotten. It could be that as the Church once wanted a "realised eschatology" it now needs a sort of "unrealised soteriology", a *reculer pour mieux sauter* in the understanding of the doctrine of Christ.

At least Christians should remember, and if they are perplexed by intellectual difficulties they may take comfort in remembering, that there is no promise that anything can be achieved hereabouts without death and resurrection: that incorporation into Christ has fundamentally to do with dying and rising with him. Finally this is to be fulfilled through physical death: those who can anticipate such fulfilment in this life will not do it by anything more morally trivial than physical death. The comfort comes from the thought that a characteristic pronoun here is "with". There is no need to comprehend the metaphysical depth of "in" before one can start to enter *with* Christ into Christ's death. Alongsideness can come before immanence and the promised indwelling is indeed promise, not condition: offered, not demanded.

INDEX